D0984020

Who Wants to Be a Jewish Writer?

Who Wants to Be a Jewish Writer?

And Other Essays

Adam Kirsch

Yale UNIVERSITY PRESS

New Haven & London

Published with assistance from the Mary Cady Tew Memorial Fund.

Yale University Press books may be purchased in quantity for educational, business, or promotional use. For information, please e-mail sales.press@yale.edu (U.S. office) or sales@yaleup.co.uk (U.K. office).

Set in Janson type by Integrated Publishing Solutions, Grand Rapids, Michigan.
Printed in the United States of America.

Library of Congress Control Number: 2018953596
ISBN 978-0-300-24013-9 (hardcover : alk. paper)

A catalogue record for this book is available from the British Library.

This paper meets the requirements of ANSI / NISO Z39.48-1992 (Permanence of Paper).

10 9 8 7 6 5 4 3 2 1

Contents

Contents

Preface

"More and more mankind will discover that we have to turn to poetry to interpret life for us, to console us, to sustain us. Without poetry, our science will appear incomplete; and most of what now passes with us for religion and philosophy will be replaced by poetry." When Matthew Arnold offered this formulation of the duty, and opportunity, of modern poetry, he was expressing a distinctively Victorian blend of optimism and despair. The sages of the nineteenth century believed that religion was on the way out of human civilization, its vision of the world made obsolete by modern science. This was a fearful prospect, since religion had always been humanity's best source of moral and metaphysical guidance. Without it, wouldn't we be set adrift, spinning in a directionless void, as Nietzsche wrote in his parable of the madman? If the beauty, mystery, and meaning of existence depend on religious belief, then a world without God would have to be as mournful as Thomas Hardy's poem "God's Funeral":

> So, toward our myth's oblivion,
> Darkling, and languid-lipped, we creep and grope
> Sadlier than those who wept in Babylon,
> Whose Zion was a still abiding hope.

But Arnold holds out the promise that humanity can learn to compensate for God's absence. After all, if God can disappear, that means he was always just a creation of human imagination; and if we could imagine God, why shouldn't we be able to imagine his replacement? For Arnold, as a not uncritical follower of the Romantic tradition of William Wordsworth and Percy Bysshe Shelley, it was poetry that offered the purest expression of human imagination. It would be up to the great poets of the future to reconcile humanity to a godless existence, by proving that such an existence could be just as rich in meaning. A new world would look to the poet not merely for new epics and lyrics, but for new myths: "We should conceive of [poetry] as capable of higher uses, and called to higher destinies, than those which in general men have assigned to it hitherto," Arnold wrote.

Almost a century and a half later, it is clear that his prediction was both right and wrong. Arnold was right that human beings cannot live without myths to console us and sustain us, but he was wrong to think that poetry would be able to supply those myths. For a myth functions only if people can believe it is true, and to call something a poem is already to relegate it to the realm of untruth, of mere imagination. The reactionary poet and critic T. E. Hulme described Romanticism, contemptuously, as "spilt religion," and religion is not usable if it is spilled; it has to be concentrated into ritual and doctrine if it is to serve any purpose. That is why the really effective myths in the twentieth century would be lies that insisted they were not lies, such as fascism and communism. And compared with those poems of the actual, the traditional religious myths that Arnold believed were obsolete start to look pretty reasonable and humane. At the very least, they preserve space for the sanctity of human life and for a recognition of mystery and limit. Perhaps that is why humanity now seems to be returning to the old monotheisms.

The result is that, in the twenty-first century, we have a situation not unlike the one Arnold knew: an educated class that is skeptical of religion, uneasily facing a majority that continues to live on terms defined by religion. And it is safe to say that poets, who in America are a subdivision of the academic intelligentsia, mainly fall on the skeptical side of this divide. There are very few poets writing traditional religious verse today, at least not in the professional literary world, and those who do tend to approach faith in the hypothetical, metaphorical fashion of liberal theologians. Poetry commands too small an audience to be able to offer the kind of sustenance and consolation Arnold believed it could provide to humanity.

But this shrinking of poetry's social mission provides, in turn, new possibilities for writers and readers. For there is still a deep affinity between poetry and religion, though today we might no longer think of it as having to do with the creative power of the imagination. Rather, what poetry and religion have in common is that they are both idioms in which we can talk seriously about the things that matter most. For this purpose, it may not be very important whether a poet believes she is talking to herself, to a small audience of readers, or to God. In his post-religious poem "Church-Going," Philip Larkin wrote that, even to an unbeliever, a church has value as "a serious house on serious earth." In the same sense, poetry is serious language, which stands on religious grounds even when it is not the work of a believer.

To think about poetry and religion in this way is implicitly to favor certain kinds of each. I have always been drawn to people, in life and on the page, for whom religion is a live issue, an open question, rather than something to be either automatically dismissed or automatically obeyed. Possibly for the same reason, the poetry that matters most to me involves a kind of personal risk, a putting of the self at stake, in ways that run deeper than autobiographical confession. I like writers who are ironical about themselves; who know that a formal statement of beliefs, religious or artistic or political, can never be fully accurate or adequate; who keep being drawn back to questions that they might have believed were answered. The essays collected in this book, written over the past decade, were not written with a program in mind, but it seems to me that they converge on the intersection of poetry and religion because these are the most available languages for discussing ultimate questions.

For me, being a Jewish writer involves a consciousness that religion and poetry also have inescapable social, historical, and political dimensions. When I write about Jewish literature, it is usually these themes that I am drawn to, rather than to strictly spiritual or theological questions. This is partly because of the nature of modern Jewish literature, which is generally on uneasy terms with traditional belief and practice. It is also due to the fact that, even in a secular Western society, Jews will often find themselves outside the mainstream, politically and intellectually, in ways that seem more significant and challenging to me over time. (Larkin wrote "Church-Going," but there is no classic English poem on "Synagogue-Going," and if there were, it would mean something very different.)

Much of my work as a critic over the past ten years has been devoted to understanding what it really means to be a Jew and a Jewish writer in such a culture. For me, this involves discovering or constructing a tradition of modern Jewish literature that can serve as a source of guidance alongside the post-Christian tradition of writers like Arnold and Hardy, which I came to know earlier in my education. In preparing this collection of essays, for instance, I found that I make repeated reference to Walter Benjamin, who stood at the center of so many of the major conflicts of Jewish modernity.

In the end, it seems to me that literature and religion and politics are parts of the same enterprise of thought. This doesn't mean that the terms of all these domains are interchangeable—that literature should be judged by its political virtue or efficacy, or that religion should be asked to provide the same kind of experience as a poem, or that politics should be encouraged to impose an aesthetic order on life. Perhaps the central responsibility of a literary critic is to know how to keep these domains separate, without forgetting that they are deeply connected: they are all ways of trying to understand what this world really is and how we are supposed to live in it.

Who Wants to Be a Jewish Writer?

Several years ago, I moderated a discussion between two novelists at the Museum of Jewish Heritage in Manhattan. The setting seemed appropriate, since these were Jewish writers who wrote about Jewish characters and themes. But when I asked them if they considered themselves Jewish novelists, both answered emphatically in the negative. They were American writers who happened to be Jewish and who happened to write about Jews, some of the time—but "Jewish writer" was a label they had no interest in.

Who could blame them? After all, Philip Roth himself once told an interviewer: "The epithet 'American Jewish writer' has no meaning for me. If I'm not an American, I'm nothing." If the author of *Goodbye, Columbus; Portnoy's Complaint; The Ghost Writer;*

and *Operation Shylock*—the most profound and obsessive books ever written about what it means to be an American Jew—does not want to be thought of as a Jewish writer, why should anyone else accept the description? And the truth is that some of the most accomplished American Jewish writers have not accepted it. Saul Bellow spoke in similar terms: "I am often described as a Jewish writer," he once wrote. "In much the same way, one might be called a Samoan astronomer or an Eskimo cellist or a Zulu Gainsborough expert. There is some oddity about it. I am a Jew, and I have written some books. I have tried to fit my soul into the Jewish-writer category, but it does not feel comfortably accommodated there."

There is, of course, one very good reason why writers would want to avoid "the Jewish-writer category": simple math. There are 320 million Americans, of whom about five million are Jewish; announcing oneself as a Jewish writer seems to cut out 98 percent of potential readers. But the math is not quite that conclusive, since it has never been true that only Jews read books by Jewish writers. Certainly, it was not true half a century ago, during what now looks like the golden age of American Jewish letters. This was a time when writers like Bellow and Bernard Malamud reached the best-seller list and won major literary prizes while writing unapologetically Jewish books such as *Herzog* and *The Magic Barrel*.

This literary moment, which lasted roughly from the 1950s to the 1970s, can be explained by a confluence of two factors. First was the decline of anti-Semitism that followed the Holocaust, which lowered the barriers of entry to the literary and academic professions and made Jews an object of sympathetic interest. Second, and probably more important, was the coming of age of the first native-born generation of American Jews—writers born in the 1910s and 1920s whose parents had come to the United States during the great wave of Eastern European immigration before World War I. For these Jews, the emphasis on textual mastery that had always defined Jewish intellectual life took on new literary forms.

That is because the Jewish immigration to America marked a profound break in the chain of transmission of Jewish texts, a chain that went back dozens of generations. In *The Rise of David Levinsky*, published in 1917 and often described as the first American Jewish novel, Abraham Cahan tells the story of a Jewish immigrant who finds his early Talmudic education slipping away from him in the new world. With an eye to the non-Jewish reader, Cahan has David Levinsky, his narrator, summarize the importance of Talmud study in Eastern European Jewish life:

> A Talmudic education was until recent years practically the only kind of education a Jewish boy of old-fashioned parents received. I spent seven years at it, not counting the several years of Talmud which I had had at the various cheders. What is the Talmud? . . . It is at once a fountain of religious inspiration and a "brain-sharpener." . . . We were sure that the highest mathematics taught in the Gentile universities were child's play as compared to the Talmud.

But the Talmud has already begun to lose its power for David before he leaves the old country. The murder of his mother by gentile neighbors drives thoughts of study from his mind and encourages him to start thinking of emigration. When he is departing for America, a rich woman who has been his sponsor meets him at the train station: "'Here,' she said, handing me a ten-ruble bill and a package. 'There is a boiled chicken in it, and some other things, provided you won't neglect your Talmud in America.'" Yet neglect it he does, inevitably. The very "brain-sharpening" that Talmud study provided helps David to acquire other, secular kinds of knowledge that prove more useful in America, such as learning English. And while he never loses his love for the Talmud, over time his connection with it is broken, as the energies that once went into textual study are employed to make a fortune in the garment business.

Accordingly, in the generation after Abraham Cahan's, the first American-born generation, it was a rare American Jewish writer who grew up with any knowledge of or fondness for Jewish study. A rare exception is Herman Wouk, who, in addition to novels like *The Caine Mutiny*, also wrote *This Is My God*, a popular introduction to Judaism. But more Jewish writers would have agreed with Lionel Trilling when he wrote: "I cannot discover anything in my professional intellectual life which I can specifically trace back to my Jewish birth and rearing. I do not think of myself as a 'Jewish writer.' I do not have it in mind to serve by my writing any Jewish purpose." Trilling connected this lack of interest in Jewishness with what seemed to him the barrenness of Judaism itself: "Modern Jewish religion at its best may indeed be intelligent and soaked in university knowledge, but out of it there has not come a single voice with the note of authority—of philosophical, or poetic, or even of rhetorical, let alone of religious, authority."

Ironically, Trilling himself would later be described, by the sociologist Philip Rieff, as the archetypal "Jew of culture": a man whose wisdom, moral seriousness, and commitment to textual study marked him as a twentieth-century version of an ancient Jewish type. Yet this Jewishness remained a matter of resemblance and form, not of content or substance. For Trilling and other Jewish critics and scholars of his generation, the intellectual ambitions that their ancestors had directed toward mastery of Jewish texts were now redirected to English and American literature. In 1942, Alfred Kazin published his first book, *On Native Grounds*, a study of American fiction. The title itself made a clear point: Jews were now natives of the United States; they belonged to American literature, and American literature belonged to them. In the decades after World War II, many of the leading critics of English and American literature were Jews, from Kazin and Trilling to Leslie Fiedler, Harry Levin, and M. H. Abrams, the creator of the *Norton Anthology of English Literature*.

This success makes it difficult to recognize how unlikely the Jewish entry into American letters once seemed. Consider how things looked to Henry James in 1904, when he paid a visit to the

Lower East Side of Manhattan, then the most densely populated Jewish neighborhood in the world. To James, the presence of so many Jews on American soil was not exactly a cause for celebration, and in *The American Scene* he wrote anxiously about what these Yiddish-speaking immigrants and their descendants would do to his beloved English language. He envisioned the American writer—which for James of course meant a writer of Anglo-Saxon stock—as a defender of the honor of English against what he called, ominously, "the Accent of the Future": "It was in the light of letters, that is in the light of our language as literature has hitherto known it, that one stared at this all-unconscious impudence of the agency of future ravage."

Far from being impudent ravagers, however, it turned out that American Jewish writers only wanted to join the English literary tradition themselves. It was Leon Edel, another Jewish scholar, who wrote James's biography in five volumes. The anti-Semitism of writers like T. S. Eliot and Ezra Pound did not stop Jews from becoming some of their greatest enthusiasts and expositors. And after World War II, when even genteel anti-Semitism fell into disrepute by association with Nazism, the WASP establishment began to reciprocate that affection. In his 1959 book *Life Studies*, Robert Lowell, whose relatives included the nineteenth-century poet James Russell Lowell and the Harvard president A. Lawrence Lowell, began an account of his family history by focusing on a very different ancestor:

The account of him is platitudinous, worldly, and fond, but he has no Christian name and is entitled merely Major M. Myers in my cousin Cassie Mason Myers Julius-James's privately printed *Biographical Sketches.* . . . The name-plate under his portrait used to spell out his name bravely enough: he was Mordecai Myers. . . . Undoubtedly Major Mordecai had lived in a more ritualistic, gaudy, and animal world than twentieth-century Boston. There was something undecided, Mediterranean, versatile, almost double-faced about his bearing. . . . He was a dark man, a German Jew. . . . In the anarchy of my adolescent war on my parents, I tried to make him a true wolf, the wandering Jew!

Clearly, whatever it was that Jewishness represented to Lowell —some kind of "gaudy and animal" alternative to proper Boston, some productive estrangement from the American norm— made it an identity worth cherishing. Indeed, by the 1970s, James's complaint had begun to change into its opposite: now, some Protestant writers felt that Jews had become only too solicitous of the honor, and the honors, of American literature. John Updike, whose chief rivals for literary glory included Bellow, Roth, J. D. Salinger, and Norman Mailer, wrote a series of books about a fictional Jewish writer called Henry Bech, which allowed him to explore and critique the sudden prominence of American Jewish novelists. "The book . . . had not so much been about a Jew as about a writer, who was a Jew with the same inevitability that a fictional rug salesman would be an Armenian," Updike explained in 1971. There is something unmistakably rude in this comparison—just ask an Armenian how he would like to be stereotyped as a rug dealer—even as it pays homage to the surprising way in which Jews had become synonymous with American literature.

Writing almost a century after James, however, Updike still clung to the idea that there was something profoundly incompatible about Jewishness and Americanness. This becomes clear in one of the last Bech stories, "Bech Noir," in which Henry Bech takes his revenge on one Orlando Cohen, a famous critic. As Cohen is dying, he uses his last breath to denounce Bech as an inauthentic writer:

> "You thought you could skip out . . . of yourself and write American. Bech . . . let me ask you. Can you say the Lord's prayer? . . . Well, ninety percent of the zhlubs around you can. It's in their heads. They can rattle . . . the damn thing right off . . . how can you expect to write about people . . . when you don't have a clue to the chozzerai . . . that's in their heads . . . they stuck it out . . . but that God-awful faith . . . Bech . . . when it burns out . . . it leaves a dead spot. That's where America is . . . in that dead spot. Em, Emily, that guy in the woods . . . Hem, Mel, Haw . . . they were there. No in thunder . . . the Big No. Jews don't know how to say No. All we know is Yes."

In a century whose most famous Jewish writer was Franz Kafka, the idea that Jews only know how to say yes is bizarre, but it goes directly to the heart of Updike's understanding of American literature. For Updike, tracing an intellectual lineage to Dickinson,

Melville, and Hawthorne, what makes literature American is a post-Protestant wrestle with the absence of a redeeming God. Jews, he suggests—as so many English professors suggested before him—cannot in their bones understand this kind of American experience. They are too this-worldly to share the American longing for transcendence. This is, of course, a recapitulation of the ancient Christian understanding, going back to the apostle Paul, that Judaism is a religion of the letter, while Christianity embraces the spirit.

In her 1976 story "Levitation," however, Cynthia Ozick, another leading American Jewish writer of this period, put a different spin on that hostile equation. The story centers on a married couple, both second-rate novelists, one Jewish and one Christian. They decide to throw a party to advance their literary careers, but fail to attract any of the A-listers they hoped for. (Notably, these are all Jewish writers and intellectuals, such as Irving Howe, Susan Sontag, and Alfred Kazin.) Instead, the focus of the gathering turns out to be an émigré professor who tells stories of his experiences in the Holocaust. As the Jewish guests flock around him, Ozick writes, something strange happens:

> The room began to ascend. It lifted. It rose like an ark on waters. Lucy said inside her mind, "This chamber of Jews." It seemed to her that the room was levitating on the little grains of the refugee's whisper. She felt herself alone at the bottom, below the floorboards, while the room floated upward, carrying Jews. Why did it not take her too?

Here it is the Jews who are spiritualized, literally rising in the air, in a Chagall-like scene, while the gentiles remain bound to the earth and the flesh. It was the Holocaust, this parable suggests, that endowed even American Jews, who did not live through it, with a kind of spiritual prestige. Auschwitz was a source of authenticity, an experience of the ultimate, before which outsiders felt bewilderment tinged by envy. There is a definite truth in Ozick's insight—just look at the way American Jewish identity, in the years since she wrote, has increasingly turned the Holocaust into a source of the sacred. But Ozick's magical-realist image can also be read in other, more skeptical ways. The levitating Jews are a pun on the Yiddish term *luftmensch*, meaning someone who lives "in the air," detached from worldly concerns like making a living. They also, of course, remind us of the fate of the Jews whose ashes were literally dispersed into the air at Auschwitz. Ozick wants us to remember that levitation—being removed from human connection and from the earth itself—is not a desirable fate, even if from some angles it looks like an interesting one.

As it happens, Ozick is the rare Jewish writer who has positively embraced a Jewish literary identity. Jewish experience, Jewish ethics, at times even Jewish theology, are the explicit subjects of most of her great fiction. Yet precisely because she does want her work to be understood as a contribution to Jewish literature, Ozick is tormented by the barriers that separate American writers from Jewish tradition. In a 1970 essay, "Toward a

New Yiddish," she provocatively wrote: "There have been no Jewish literary giants in Diaspora. There are no major works of Jewish imaginative genius written in any Gentile language, sprung out of any Gentile culture." By this, Ozick does not mean that there have been no great Jewish writers in non-Jewish languages: she knows Kafka and Bellow as well as anyone. Rather, she meant that when Jews write in non-Jewish languages, they no longer possess a specifically Jewish imagination.

This is an idea redolent of nineteenth-century nationalism, which celebrated the mystic bond between nation, language, and writer. It is an unfamiliar idea in America, where the exchange of the ancestral language for English is a rite of passage for immigrant writers. But in Jewish tradition, the idea that language—specifically, the Hebrew language—is an integral part of Jewish existence has very deep roots. For instance, in the Talmud, in Tractate Sota, the rabbis debate whether it is possible to address God in Aramaic, which in their time was the daily language of most Jews. According to Rabbi Yochanan, it is not possible, because "the ministering angels are not familiar with the Aramaic language."

But other rabbis note that, on one occasion, the Voice of God was heard to deliver a message to the High Priest in the Holy of Holies, and that voice spoke Aramaic. The fact is that, starting with the Babylonian Exile, Hebrew has always been a foreign language to large segments of the Jewish people. The Gemara itself is written in Aramaic. Many Greek-speaking Jews in the

Roman Empire knew the Bible only in the Greek translation known as the Septuagint; this was true of Philo of Alexandria, the biblical commentator. These Jews cherished the legend that, when King Ptolemy of Egypt imported seventy translators to render the Bible from Hebrew into Greek, each of the seventy emerged from seclusion having produced the exact same text— proof that the Septuagint was divinely inspired and perfect, just like the original. Again, Maimonides's *Guide of the Perplexed*, the greatest work of medieval Jewish philosophy, was written in Judeo-Arabic.

So Ozick is wrong to insist that Jewish literature cannot exist outside of a Jewish language. Still, it is surely true that English is more like Greek than it is like Hebrew, Aramaic, and Yiddish, the primary Jewish languages of the past. English is a world language, in which Jews will never make up more than a tiny percentage of speakers. It has no roots in Jewish tradition or text. Equally important, it will never be a language in which Jews can talk to one another without the outside world listening in. To write in English, even about Jewish subjects, is necessarily to exchange one's place in an exclusively Jewish literary tradition for a place in the much more diverse and cosmopolitan tradition of English literature.

For most American Jewish writers, this seems like a very good trade. Certainly it represents a vast increase in potential readership, which is why Hebrew writers gain more from translation into English than vice versa. Yet there are other kinds of gains than sheer numbers. That is the point of an anecdote that Bellow once told about his meeting in Jerusalem with S. Y. Agnon, the only Hebrew writer to receive the Nobel Prize in Literature. Agnon asked Bellow if his own books had ever been translated into Hebrew: "If they had not been, he had better see to it immediately because, he said, they would survive only in the Holy Tongue." When Bellow replied that Heinrich Heine seemed to have a pretty secure reputation despite writing in German, Agnon responded that Heine was safe, since he had already been translated into Hebrew.

This was a joke, but a pointed one. The number of people in the world who understand Hebrew is small—there are about five million native speakers in Israel, and perhaps four million Jews elsewhere who know the language with varying degrees of fluency. That's about the same as the population of New York City or Sweden. English, on the other hand, is the native language of about 400 million people, and a second language for a billion others, including many Israelis. It seems, to put it mildly, counterintuitive to say that a Hebrew text stands a better chance of survival than an English one. Yet the same thing could have been said of Latin two thousand years ago, and who speaks Latin today? The earliest Hebrew texts have been read and circulated for some three thousand years, and the core of the Jewish prayer service is substantially the same today as it was when the Temple stood in Jerusalem. When words are lodged deeply enough in the heart of a people, they can stay alive for a fantastically long time, and against great odds. Who knows if anyone will be reading Agnon or Bellow in five hundred years' time; but if they are, it's certainly possible that they will be reading them in Hebrew.

Of course, it is not a calculation on posterity that determines what language a writer uses, or what he or she writes about. The first decision, about language, is usually made for us: we write the language we have grown up speaking. For American Jewish writers, that means English. Hebrew can be acquired, but only with great effort starting at an early age—which means, in practical terms, that it is acquired only by people with a strong religious background, or a strong ideological incentive, like the early Zionists. Most young American Jews are lucky if they learn enough Hebrew to follow the prayer service. In my own case, although I went to Hebrew school programs from the age of five to eighteen, I started college without knowing enough Hebrew to ask directions, not to mention read Amos Oz. I would have had to start my education over in a much more rigorous way if I was to achieve the ability to read Hebrew literature, and by then it was too late for me to hope to write it.

The reason it didn't even occur to me to make that choice has to do with the second decision every writer faces: what to write about. This, too, is usually made for us, though in a different way. In my case, being a writer, a poet, was what I hoped for starting as a teenager. But being a Jewish writer would have seemed to me, at that stage of life, to be nothing but a limitation. When I look back and try to understand why this was, I remember how

I felt about the poetry that inspired me at that time. This was American, English, sometimes French. But its subject was not religious or ethnic or national experience; it was universal, human experience. To ask what this poetry had to do with being Jewish would have made as much sense to me as asking what the taste of pepper had to do with the length of a mile—to borrow a comparison Maimonides uses in the *Guide of the Perplexed*. Jewishness was a circumscribed part of life, having to do with going to synagogue, going to Hebrew school, keeping dietary laws, and other such discrete activities. The source of poetry went much deeper into what it meant to be alive.

Something like this is what American Jewish writers are trying to express when they shun the label of Jewish writer. Writing, they mean to say, is about the fundamentals of life, things everybody can understand: love, hate, fear, desire, beauty. To call oneself a Jewish writer might seem to imply that one loves, hates, and so on in a different way from people who are not Jewish, and of course this is not the case, any more than it is the case with any ethnic or religious distinction. Yet with other kinds of identity, it is taken for granted that the local is not in conflict with the universal, but is precisely the way to reach the universal. When Joyce wrote about Dublin or Faulkner wrote about the American South, they didn't anxiously insist that they were not Irish or Southern writers, just writers. They knew that it was only by describing a particular way of life with great specificity that they could make it meaningful, even to people who led very different lives.

Why do so many Jewish writers not feel the same way? One possible answer is that they do feel the same way, they just don't want to admit it. After all, there have been few more carefully detailed milieus in American fiction than Roth's Jewish Newark or Bellow's Jewish Chicago. As writers, they knew that the Jewishness of their experience was identical to its humanness, not in competition with it. Take, for instance, a passage from Roth's novel *Portnoy's Complaint*, where he describes football games at Weequahic High, the Jewish neighborhood school in Newark, whose fans would chant:

> Ikey, Mikey, Jake and Sam,
> We're the boys who eat no ham,
> We play football, we play soccer—
> And we keep matzohs in our locker!
> Aye, aye, aye, Weequahic High!

"So what if we had lost?" Roth continues. "It turned out we had other things to be proud of. We ate no ham. We kept matzohs in our lockers. Not really, of course, but if we wanted to we could, and we weren't ashamed to say that we actually did! We were Jews—and we weren't ashamed to say it! We were Jews—and not only were we not inferior to the goyim who beat us at football, but the chances were that because we could not commit our hearts to victory in such a thuggish game, we were superior! . . . And what made us superior was precisely the hatred and the disrespect they lavished so willingly upon us!"

There is no shying away from Jewishness here. Roth frankly

lays out the psychic convolutions of being Jewish in 1940s America, the dialectic of superiority and inferiority, pride and shame. He does so with the expectation that any reader, Jewish or not, will be able to understand, and even sympathize with, this parochial phenomenon. Indeed, that was the great daring of Roth's fiction, a daring that went too far for some of his Jewish critics. Yet somehow the name of Jewish writer still felt to him like a restriction, a deprivation.

The only way to explain this is to reckon with the ambiguous role that Jewishness plays in the lives of modern Jews, especially in America. This ambiguity is the product of our successful assimilation, which historically speaking is a recent and anomalous phenomenon. Jews in America do not speak a Jewish language, as our ancestors did; we don't live in exclusively Jewish communities, as our ancestors did; the majority of us do not observe Jewish laws, as our ancestors did. That last difference is the most significant from a religious perspective, but perhaps the least important from a literary perspective. Look, for instance, at the Israeli poet Yehuda Amichai, who was born in Germany as Ludwig Pfeuffer and came to pre-state Israel as a teenager. Because he was an Israeli writing a Hebrew full of biblical allusions, no one would hesitate to assign his work to Jewish literature, even though many of Amichai's subjects would seem entirely secular if treated by an American Jew in English.

Unless, of course, the writer in question had made Jewishness a central element in his or her work in general. In that case, the text might exfoliate with Jewish meanings in unexpected ways—perhaps even in ways unexpected by the writer himself. Jewishness in American literature, that is, turns out to have the same elusive and perspectival quality that it has in American life. The same person might feel not at all Jewish when alone in a forest, and very Jewish when in a synagogue—or vice versa. He might feel most Jewish when taking pride in Israel or when boycotting Israel. It is because American Jewishness is no longer a simple fact of language, community, or belief that it has become a matter of feeling. This might seem like an insubstantial kind of Jewishness, and perhaps it is. But it is the truth of American Jewish life, and any honest literary depiction of that life has to include it. In this sense, an American Jewish writer's denial of Jewishness can be considered a deeply expressive Jewish act.

The Book of Psalms

"Whatever David says in his book pertains to himself, to all Israel, and to all times," declares Midrash Tehillim, the early rabbinic commentary on the book of Psalms. If the rabbis erred, it was not on the side of exaggeration; for it is not just Israel that placed the Psalms at the center of its spiritual vocabulary. These one hundred and fifty poems, traditionally ascribed to King David, had a definite but now unclear function in the rituals of the Temple in Jerusalem. After the Temple was destroyed, they migrated to the Jewish prayer service, where they are ubiquitous. To this day, Psalms is the book to which the devout most often turn, in joy and in sorrow.

But it was Christianity that managed to disseminate the Psalms throughout Europe and the world, on a scale that their authors could never have imagined. In the Middle Ages, the Liturgy of the Hours consisted of eight daily services, each centered on the singing of a psalm, and monks took it upon themselves to recite the entire Latin Psalter every week. With the Reformation, these poems and hymns gained even larger audiences as they were translated into the European vernaculars. The Anglican Book of Common Prayer included the King James Version of the Psalter and provided for the full cycle to be read monthly, as well as assigning appropriate Psalms to each holiday. It is fair to say that as a result, from the sixteenth century through the twentieth, no lyrics were more widely or deeply read in Europe than the Psalms. For a reader of English literature, knowing the King James Psalter is as indispensable as knowing Shakespeare or Mother Goose.

It is not just the sheer familiarity of the Psalms, however, that explains their extraordinary influence. These Hebrew texts, which scholars now believe were written by a series of anonymous poets between 1000 and 400 BCE, seemed to generations of readers to be the very scripts of their own inner lives. Martin Luther, who translated the Psalter into German and used it as the basis for his hymns, wrote that "this book, though small, deserves to be recommended above all others," since even for the ordinary, theologically unenlightened Christian it offered "some little sweetness of the breath of life, and some small taste of consolation, like the faint fragrance which is found in the air not far from a bed of roses." John Donne echoed the sentiment in a sermon preached at St. Paul's Cathedral in 1625. "The Psalms are the Manna of the Church," he proposed. "As Manna tasted to every man like that that he liked best, so do the Psalms minister instruction, and satisfaction, to every man, in every emergency and occasion."

From their different theological and historical perspectives, such commentators converged on the idea that the Psalms were uniquely suited for what we would now call appropriation. They could be taken over and used in equally valid ways by Jews, Catholics, and Protestants, in Hebrew, Latin, or English; indeed, Providence had designed them for that very purpose. But the Christian appropriation of the Psalms was also inevitably a kind of confiscation, and the way Luther or Donne read the poems was partly to misread them. The process is already at work in Donne's phrase "the Manna of the Church," as though the Psalms were Christian texts that only sojourned among the Jews until the true church was ready to receive them. "David," as Donne put it, "was not only a clear Prophet of Christ himself, but a Prophet of every particular Christian."

This assumption was crucial to the way King James's committee of scholars, and subsequent Christian translators, turned the Psalms into English. If the Psalms were essentially a Christian text, then it was not just legitimate but imperative to employ a Christian theological vocabulary of sin and soul and salvation. And that vocabulary, which for English readers became the very language of the Psalms, itself sanctioned the belief that the Psalmist thought in Christian concepts. Take Psalm 2, which reads, in the King James Version: "I will declare the decree: the Lord hath said unto me, Thou art my Son; this day have I begotten thee." Elsewhere in the Psalm, it is clear that the speaker of this line is a king of Israel, and that the divine power he claims is the ability to defeat his foes in battle: "Thou shalt break them with a rod of iron; thou shalt dash them in pieces like a potter's vessel." Yet the text virtually insists that we take the "Son" to be Jesus. Not only is the noun capitalized, so is the pronoun, and the word "begotten" comes straight out of the Nicene Creed ("I believe . . . in one Lord Jesus Christ, the only begotten Son of God").

The translators' work of Christianizing the Psalms was not always so blatant. In Psalm 23, possibly the best known of all the King James versions, the third verse begins, "He restoreth my soul." Inevitably the phrase makes us think of resurrection, and it turns the Psalmist's imagery of "green pastures" and "still waters" into metaphors for heaven. By the time we reach the end of the poem—"and I will dwell in the house of the Lord for ever"—it is impossible to read "for ever" as meaning anything but "eternally," in the time-without-end of the redeemed soul.

One of the tasks that Robert Alter undertakes in his translation of the Psalms is to evacuate the covert theological assumptions of the Authorized Version. "The pointed absence of 'soul' and 'salvation'" from his English version, Alter notes, are only the most obvious signs of this program. It extends even to capitalization, as can be seen in his version of Psalm 2. Where the King James Version has "Thou art my Son," leaving no doubt that the second person belongs to the Second Person of the Trinity, Alter has "You are My son," restricting the honorific capital to the speaker. Again, in Psalm 23, in place of "He restoreth my soul," Alter's version reads "My life He brings back": "the Hebrew *nefesh*," Alter explains, "does not mean 'soul' but 'life breath' or 'life.'" In the same poem, Alter's Psalmist concludes by asking to live in the house of the Lord not "for ever" but "for many long days"—the true meaning of the Hebrew *l'orech yamim*. "The viewpoint of the poem," his note explains, "is in and of the here and now and is in no way eschatological."

The combined effect of these changes is to remove the Psalms from the Christian drama of sin and redemption, and to situate them firmly in this world. This does not mean that Alter's Psalms automatically become a more Jewish text—a point worth emphasizing, because the equation of Christianity with the transcendent and Judaism with the immanent is an old trope of Christian apologetics. In his *Reflections on the Psalms*, for instance, C. S. Lewis opined that the Psalmist's constant appeal for God's judgment against his enemies is "very characteristically Jewish": "the Christian pictures the case to be tried as a criminal case with himself in the dock; the Jew pictures it as a civil case with himself as the plaintiff. The one hopes for acquittal, or rather for pardon; the other hopes for a resounding triumph with heavy damages."

It is good to have an English version of the Psalms that is liberated from this sort of interpretation. For the truth is that

Alter's systematic return to the original Hebrew text leaves his Psalms estranged from the ethical language of both Judaism and Christianity. "We are all accustomed to think of Psalms, justifiably, as a religious book," he writes, "but its religious character is not the same as that of the Christian and Jewish traditions that variously evolved over the centuries after the Bible." Instead of looking forward to their "fulfillment" in some messianic antitype, Alter's Psalms look backward—to the warrior culture that produced them, obsessed with honor, shame, and revenge, and even to the polytheistic Canaanite mythology that lurked in the background of Israelite religion. Psalm 95 declares: "For a great god is the Lord, / and great king over all the gods," and in Psalm 104 we find God making war on the Ocean, as Baal did on the sea-god Yam in Canaanite myth:

> over mountains the waters stood.
> From Your blast they fled, from the sound of Your thunder they
>   scattered.
> They went up the mountains, went down the valleys, to the
>   place that You founded for them.
> A border You fixed so they could not cross, so they could not
>   come back to cover the earth.

But polytheism is only a trace element in the Psalms. More disconcerting, because more fundamental, is the ethical ambiguity of their monotheism. The Psalmist appears in several guises over the course of these one hundred and fifty poems: as the awed observer of the Creation ("The heavens tell God's glory, /

and His handiwork sky declares"); as the chronicler of Jewish history ("I found David my servant, / with My holy oil anointed him"); as the ecstatic celebrant of God's attributes ("Greatness and grandeur before Him, / strength and splendor in His sanctuary"). But he is most frequently to be found approaching God as a supplicant, requesting divine help against the enemies that surround him.

The ground of his prayer, almost always, is justice. He deserves God's help because he is righteous and pious, while his enemies are the reverse. Thus Psalm 73:

> They mock and speak with malice, from on high they speak out
>   oppression.
> They put their mouth up to the heavens, and their tongue goes
>   over the earth.
> Thus the people turn back to them, and they lap up their
>   words.
> And they say, "How could God know, and is there knowledge
>   with the Most High?"
> Look, such are the wicked. . . .

In this way, the Psalmist merges ethics and faith until they become a single entity: if to believe in God is to believe in a good God, then to do evil is implicitly to deny God. "The scoundrel has said in his heart, / There is no God,'" as Alter renders the famous beginning of Psalm 14.

Yet this equation of faith with goodness, which gives the Psalms their ethical sublimity, can also be read in the other direction.

For if God is called upon to punish evildoers not just because they do evil, but primarily because they disbelieve in Him, then God's motives are not exactly disinterested. Doing justice becomes a way of defending God's honor, rather than a categorical imperative, and so the ideal of justice is ironized even as it is affirmed. This logic explains why the Psalmist can sometimes sound almost like Iago, insinuating that God owes it to himself to destroy his enemies, who also happen to be the speaker's enemies. "Until when, O God, will the foe insult, / the enemy revile Your name forever?" he asks in Psalm 74. "Arise, God, O plead Your cause. / Remember the insult to You by the base all day long." Such passages continue the tradition, begun by Moses, of appealing to God's interest in his own reputation.

It makes sense for the Psalmist to believe that God would respond to this sort of inveigling, because his values are those of a warrior culture, in which nothing is worse than public humiliation. Like Achilles, with whom the earliest kings of Israel were perhaps contemporary, the Psalmist believes that the acme of suffering is to see your enemies gloat over you. "In this I shall know You desire me — / that my enemy not trumpet his conquest of me," he tells God in Psalm 41. Again, in Psalm 25, he begs, "Guard my life and save me. / Let me be not shamed, for I shelter in You."

By the same token, the sweetest pleasure is to glory in the defeat of one's enemy. Nothing in the Psalms is more disturbing than the undisguised glee that the poet takes in the physical suffering of his foes, both personal and national. It is not just that he pleads with God, "Pay them back for their acts, / and for the evil of their schemings." Again like the author of the *Iliad,* the Psalmist delights in graphic images of revenge: "break the arm of the wicked," "the teeth of the wicked You smash," "That your foot may wade in blood, / the tongues of your dogs lick the enemies." The most extreme example comes at the end of Psalm 137, whose affecting opening lines—"By Babylon's streams, / there we sat, oh we wept, / when we recalled Zion"—are quoted much more often than its last lines: "Daughter of Babylon the despoiler, / happy who pays you back in kind, / for what you did to us. / Happy who seizes and smashes / your infants against the rock."

There is no denying that this violent strain is one of the reasons the Psalms have been so readily adoptable by all kinds of believers. Self-righteousness and vengefulness are some of the most seductive emotions, and the Psalms are poems that not only memorably express them but positively authorize them. It is no wonder that they have appealed in particular to masters of theological ire such as Luther and Milton, each of whom belonged to a beleaguered Christian sect. In Milton's translation of Psalm 5, the Psalmist's cause becomes the Puritan cause: "All workers of iniquity / Thou hat'st; and them unblest / Thou wilt destroy that speak a lie; / The bloody and guileful man God doth detest. / But I will in thy mercies dear / Thy numerous mercies go / Into thy house."

If this were the only voice of the Psalms, their appeal would be strong but narrow, when in fact it is strong and broad. That is because "the Psalmist," traditionally identified with King David, is a fiction. There is not just one mind at work in the Psalms, but several, and this allows the book to compass many modes of spiritual experience. That is why the Psalms can continue to speak to readers who no longer believe in their Davidic authorship or in their divine inspiration, or indeed in the biblical God. Past ages looked to these poems for expressions of their own reverence or awe or embattled righteousness, and found them. Today we may look to the Psalms for expressions of our own doubt and fear and homesickness for God, and also find them.

Indeed, the rhetorical logic of the poems requires that they confront God's distance as well as his nearness. The Psalmist's supplications, his constant demands for "rescue" (the word by which Alter translates *yeshuah*, in preference to the King James Version's "salvation"), are necessary only because his suffering was allowed to happen in the first place, by a God who is always initially absent. The most moving Psalms are those in which this tension is heightened to the point of despair, such as the well-known Psalm 42:

> As a deer yearns for streams of water,
> so I yearn for You, O God.
> My whole being thirsts for God,
> for the living God.
> When shall I come and see
> the presence of God?

It is because the Psalms make room for the experience of abjection and devastation that they continue to be appropriated by
poets who find the only evidence of God's existence in the sensation of his absence. Paul Celan has as much right to title a
poem "Psalm" as Milton did, since Celan's doubt is as true to
the spirit of the Psalms as Milton's certainty: "No one kneads
us again out of earth and clay, / no one incants our dust. / No
one. / Blessed art thou, No One."

At the same time, Alter's version reminds us that reading the
Psalms as poetry can never be the same experience as reading
them as Scripture. Surprisingly, perhaps, the difference is most
obvious not in the language of Alter's Psalms, but in their music,
which breaks just as deliberately with the expectations bred in
English readers by the Authorized Version. The verse of the King
James Psalms, while instantly recognizable, is not actually verse
at all, but highly rhythmic prose. As in the Hebrew, most lines
are composed of two versets, which balance each other semanti-
cally and syntactically. But the English version does not attempt
to match the rhythms of the Hebrew, and each line is permitted
to stretch to as many syllables as needed to capture the sense.
The resulting rhythm—as regular as systole and diastole, as lei-
surely as rocking from foot to foot—is the perfect English vehicle for the Psalms' message of reassurance. In almost every line,
the first verset seems to advance a proposition that the second
verset confirms. "Though an host should encamp against me, my
heart shall not fear: though war should rise against me, in this

will I be confident," says Psalm 27, and simply saying the words aloud seems to instill that confidence.

More than anything else, it is this primal rhythm of affirmation that makes the Psalms psalm-like to an English reader. The best proof of this is the way all other attempts to put the Psalms into English verse seem deficient when placed side by side with the King James Version. This is not to say that they are bad poetry. In the seventeenth century, some of the best English poets translated the Psalms, in versions that display all the wit and grace we associate with the golden age of English lyric. Thomas Carew usually figures in the anthologies as a minor Metaphysical poet, but his version of Psalm 91 shows how the Metaphysical idiom, with its unadorned syntax, quick leaps of imagery, and unlikely epithets, can provide an excellent vehicle for the Psalmist's message:

> Make the great God thy fort, and dwell
> In him by faith, and do not care
> (So shaded) for the power of hell
> Or for the cunning fowler's snare
> Or poison of the infected air. . . .
> The winged plague that flies by night,
> The murdering sword that kills by day,
> Shall not thy peaceful sleeps affright
> Though on thy right and left hand they
> A thousand and ten thousand slay.

This is a good poem, but it does not feel like a Psalm. The reason is that the very artfulness of the poem—the easy rhymes,

the striking adjectives, all the ways Carew leaves his own mark
and the mark of his school on it—detracts from the assured,
impersonal music of the Psalms as we know them from the Authorized Version:

> I will say of the Lord, He is my refuge and my fortress: my
> God; in him will I trust.
> Surely he shall deliver thee from the snare of the fowler, and
> from the noisome pestilence. . . .
> Thou shalt not be afraid for the terror by night; nor for the
> arrow that flieth by day;
> Nor for the pestilence that walketh in darkness; nor for the
> destruction that wasteth at noonday.
> A thousand shall fall at thy side, and ten thousand at thy right
> hand; but it shall not come nigh thee.

When the King James Version says that the godly man is in-
vincible, it sounds like a promise; when Carew says it, it sounds
like a conceit. That is why the rhythm of the King James Version
is so ideally suited to the Psalms as Scripture: its music is as affirmative as its message. It constitutes a convincing reply to the
question asked in Psalm 137: "How can we sing a song of the
Lord / on foreign soil?" Indeed, the King James Psalms deserve
to be thought of as more than just renderings of the Hebrew
Psalms. They are translations in the sense Walter Benjamin meant
when he wrote that every work has "an intention . . . which no
single language can attain by itself," which only translation into
another language can bring to light. Benjamin's conception, which
sounds merely fanciful when applied to secular literature, is per-

fectly suited to Scripture, which is in fact its true ground and inspiration. Only a divine author can have a meaning so vast that all languages are needed to convey it.

If the Psalms are a holy book, then the King James translation is canonical in more than a metaphorical sense. Not just its language and its music, but its historical role—its influence during the centuries when the Bible was a central element in English literature—endows it with an authority that no other English translation can match. Robert Alter's translation challenges that authority, by showing that the Psalms can come into English in a different form, and a more accurate one. He does this, above all, by taking aim at the central element in the canonical power of the King James Version: its rhythm. Rather than accept that this rhythm defines the psalm-like for the English reader, Alter derides it, in his introduction, as "the beauty of a proto-Whitmanesque line of poetry rather than of biblical poetry." His own "preoccupation with rhythm" means that he wants to make an English version that hews as closely as possible to the sound of the Hebrew, "emulating its rhythms wherever feasible."

Yet this ambition, reasonable as it appears, soon runs up against the reality that the sound values of one language are never convertible into those of another language. A French alexandrine cannot be converted into an English line of twelve syllables and still retain the classical symmetry and balance of the original; a six-foot line, in English, sounds like doggerel, and tends to decompose. Iambic pentameter has fewer beats and syllables than the alexandrine, but in effect it is the true English equivalent. And the sound values of Hebrew and English are, of course, still more incommensurable. Hebrew is a highly inflected language that indicates case, tense, and number through suffixes and prefixes. As a result, a given line of Hebrew almost always uses fewer words and fewer syllables than its English equivalent.

In his introduction, Alter gives the famous example of the fourth verse of Psalm 23, which the King James Version renders, "Yea, though I walk through the valley of the shadow of death, I will fear no evil." This uses seventeen words and twenty syllables of English to translate eight words and eleven syllables of Hebrew. To Alter, this expansion is a distortion, and the quality for which he most strives in his Psalms is concision. His version of the same verse reads: "Though I walk in the vale of death's shadow, I fear no harm"—thirteen words and fourteen syllables, just about splitting the difference between the Hebrew and the Authorized Version.

Yet it is questionable whether this compression makes Alter's English sound more like Hebrew. The whole point of the Hebrew, after all, is that it is not compressed—it takes exactly as many syllables as it needs and no fewer. If Alter's English seems to take fewer syllables than it needs, the result is sometimes an impression of terseness. Thus "vale" is a shorter word than "valley," but also a more anachronistic and literary one. "Death's shadow" is shorter than "the valley of the shadow of death," but also harder to say. Alter's line also demonstrates his tendency to fall into a dactylic pattern—a meter that in English sounds percussive and hurried-up, in a way that is not necessarily reflective of the original Hebrew.

If Alter's Psalms are not as beautiful as the King James Version, however, they do not have to be. His goal is not really to replace the texts we know but to estrange them, to remind us that the English Psalter conceals the Hebrew one as well as reveals it. We never forget, with Alter's Psalms, that the text we are reading is the work of human hands. There is just one exception to this estranging and secularizing program, and it is a highly suggestive one. Like all previous translators, Alter refuses to translate the name of God as "Yahweh," the imprecise English equivalent of the way the Hebrew might be pronounced. Instead he substitutes "the Lord," the equivalent of the Hebrew euphemism *Adonai*.

In this, Alter defers to the ancient Jewish ban on speaking God's name aloud, but also to the expectations of the English reader. The name Yahweh, he writes, "might run the risk of sounding as though it belonged in the *Journal of Biblical Literature*, not in a poem." Yet this is tacitly to admit what Alter's translation sets out to deny—that the Psalms cannot, and should not, be translated with the same detachment that we would bring to any other ancient text. After all, no translator would think of observing Canaanite or Egyptian taboos when turning those religions' documents into English. If even Alter feels compelled to call God "the Lord," it is not out of piety, but out of a sense that this honorific is a last remaining sign of our culture's intimate and reverent relationship with the Bible. Yahweh is the strange-sounding name of an ancient Middle Eastern deity, like Baal or Ishtar; but the Lord is the name of God. Not until God is no longer the Lord will it be possible to have a perfectly scholarly translation of the Psalms. But on that day we may no longer need the Psalms, or understand them.

Seamus Heaney and
the Question of Goodness

"Remote on the one hand from the banal, on the other from the eccentric, his genius was calculated to win at once the adhesion of the general public and the admiration, both sympathetic and stimulating, of the connoisseur." So writes Thomas Mann about Gustav von Aschenbach, great writer and national institution, in *Death in Venice*; and the description applies unexpectedly well to Seamus Heaney. Heaney was in obvious ways unlike Mann's Apollonian aesthete, but he too managed to win the love of the many and the esteem of the few, in a way that no American poet has done since Robert Frost. As Heaney observes in *Stepping Stones*, a book-length interview published in 2008 and designed to serve in lieu of a memoir, "In the United States, there's a great crop of ripe, waving poetry—but there's no monster hogweed sticking up out of it." For most of his adult life, Heaney was that hogweed in the small but teeming field of Irish poetry, and he led the richly burdened existence of the responsible artist.

"What I've said before, only half in joke, is that everybody in Ireland is famous," Heaney modestly remarks to Dennis O'Driscoll, his interlocutor in *Stepping Stones*. "Or, maybe better say everybody is familiar. Since I was a schoolboy, I've been used to being recognized on the road by old and young, and being bantered with and indeed being taunted." But of course few people in Ireland were as famous as Heaney, and few poets, in an age when poetry is benignly neglected across the English-speaking world, have so conscientiously integrated their public and poetic selves. At one point, O'Driscoll asks Heaney about the publication history of "Anything Can Happen," a post-9/11 poem based on a Horatian ode. Before it was included in his book *District and Circle*, the poem "appeared first in *The Irish Times*; then you introduced it in a lecture to the Royal College of Surgeons and published it in *Translation Ireland*; finally you republished it . . . in a booklet in support of Amnesty International."

The reason for this recycling, Heaney explains, is "ongoing civic service, I suppose. The requests for contributions to different series and different causes is unending." And "for better or worse, I was never a person who preserved myself for my writing. In fact, I do believe that your vocation puts you in line for a

certain amount of community service, so to speak." Again Aschenbach comes to mind, in Mann's description:

> Almost before he was out of high school he had a name. Ten
> years later he had learned to sit at his desk and sustain and live
> up to his growing reputation, to write gracious and pregnant
> phrases in letters that must needs be brief, for many claims
> press upon the solid and successful man. At forty, worn down
> by the strains and stresses of his actual task, he had to deal
> with a daily post heavy with tributes from his own and foreign
> countries.

Heaney was not yet forty years old when Robert Lowell pro-
claimed him "the best Irish poet since W. B. Yeats," but already
he was no stranger to anointings. The oldest of nine children, he
grew up on a farm in Northern Ireland, and the labors and plea-
sures of rural life gave him an inexhaustible subject. At the age
of twelve, Heaney was sent off to a Catholic boarding school, St.
Columb's College, whereupon "I shifted," he recalls, "into a kind
of separateness, but also a kind of privilege." "I was being 'educated,' and that meant being set a bit apart."

The separateness would only deepen as his career progressed.
In 1965, Heaney's first collection, *Death of a Naturalist*, was accepted by Faber and Faber, the premier publisher of poetry in
the English language, whose list also included Eliot and Auden.
In 1975, *North*, his collection of poems inspired by Northern
Ireland's Troubles, made his name known across the English-
speaking world. In 1982 he received the first of many honorary

degrees and became a professor at Harvard. At every stage, life vindicated the intuition of giftedness that he expresses in "The Diviner," a poem from his first book:

The bystanders would ask to have a try.
He handed them the rod without a word.
It lay dead in their grasp till, nonchalantly,
He gripped expectant wrists. The hazel stirred.

By the time Heaney won the Nobel Prize in 1995, he had long experience of the "claims [that] press upon the solid and successful man." Perhaps the most intriguing thing about Heaney, however, is how impossible it is to imagine him finally cracking under this burden of responsibility, the way Aschenbach spectacularly does. When Heaney learned that he had won the Nobel Prize, he was away in Greece, in the sensual south—not with any Tadzio, but with Marie, his wife of thirty years and the addressee of his moving, unillusioned love poems. (When his son told him the news over the phone, the first thing he said was, "You'd better tell your mother.") And he encountered the prize not as a holiday, but as another onrush of obligations: "I was in a sweat, literally and figuratively. I couldn't think clearly, because suddenly there were a dozen things to be done."

This is a truly Mann-like response to fame: the supreme conscientiousness, the duty to art and nation coming before egoistic pleasure. Mann would certainly have appreciated the image of writerly obligation that Heaney offers in "Weighing In": "And this is all the good tidings amount to: / This principle of bearing, bearing up / And bearing out." Yet Mann took revenge in his work on the "principle of bearing" that made the work possible. His fictional avatars are always collapsing under their self-imposed burdens—contracting a deadly illness, or falling in love with exotic women or boys, or committing suicide. As a result, the outward respectability of Mann's own life came to look like the most exquisite irony of all. Goodness, he seems to suggest by example, is a role, even a pretense. The more admirable the writer, the more costly his concealment.

The strength, and the enigma, of Heaney's work is that he never distances himself from his own goodness in this way. The responsibilities he sought or accepted over a long life—as son, husband, father, artist, Catholic, national conscience—are the major subjects of his verse; but if they are weights, they are never intolerable ones. They are rather, as another image from "Weighing In" has it, like the weights on a balance. And the desire to hold, or to be, the balance between competing claims and impulses can be seen in every phase of Heaney's work—for instance, in the titles of his major critical works, *The Redress of Poetry* and *The Government of the Tongue*. Other poets would have used "and" in those titles, to emphasize the tension between redress and poetry, government and the tongue—both restatements of the pair of opposites Yeats called "reality and justice." "They have helped me to hold in a single thought reality and justice" was Yeats's justification for the mystical schemes of *A Vision*, and the obsessive, outlandish detail of his system is an index of how much pressure it took to keep those opposites yoked together.

For Heaney, however, the "and" of tension gives way to the "of" of reconciliation. The golden tongue of the poet, one might suppose, is helpless before the leaden weight of power. As Heaney acknowledges, "In one sense the efficacy of poetry is nil—no lyric has ever stopped a tank." But he goes on to insist that "in another sense, it is unlimited. It is like the writing in the sand in the face of which accusers and accused are left speechless and renewed." The allusion is to the moment in the New Testament when Jesus, confronting a crowd that wants to stone a woman taken in adultery, "stooped down, and wrote on the ground, as though he heard them not," before issuing the challenge, "He that is without sin among you, let him first cast a stone at her." We do not know what Jesus was writing on the ground, nor, Heaney implies, does it matter. What matters is the fact of writing, which "holds attention for a space, functions not as distraction but as pure concentration, a focus where our power to concentrate is concentrated back on ourselves."

Heaney's parable attempts to recover for poetry the ethical and political force that Auden famously denied it when he wrote that "poetry makes nothing happen." Heaney is much too experienced a writer to believe that poetry can make something happen. But instead of lamenting poetry's nothingness, he chooses to redeem it through metaphor, turning it into an empty "space," a "focus," where it can produce spiritual—which is to say, actual—

effects. This is perhaps the best case that can still be made for the edifying value of art. And it proceeds, in typically Heaneyesque fashion, not by weighing in on either side of an old antithesis—the beautiful versus the good—but by reconciling them in a tentative synthesis: beauty sponsors goodness. Heaney admires Czesław Miłosz because "his intellect wasn't forced to choose between 'perfection of the life or of the work'—it was forced to meld them." In his belief in the reconcilability of poetry with goodness, Heaney is perhaps Miłosz's greatest disciple.

Yet it is possible to admire the nobility and the ingenuity of Heaney's reconciliations without assenting to them. Does poetry really have the function of "concentrating" us on ourselves, of shocking us out of our prejudices, the way Jesus shocked the stone-throwers? (And is that, in fact, what the Gospel story describes?) Do we return from "To Autumn," or "Lycidas," or "The Emperor of Ice-Cream" better equipped to make moral decisions? Consider even a poem explicitly concerned with political ethics, such as Heaney's "Viking Dublin: Trial Pieces":

> I am Hamlet the Dane,
> skull-handler, parablist,
> smeller of rot
> in the state, infused
> with its poisons,
> pinioned by ghosts
> and affections,
> murders and pieties,
> coming to consciousness

by jumping in graves,
dithering, blathering.

What this poem powerfully does is to capture the confusion
and oppression of political violence. It is able to do this because
of Heaney's mastery of the seemingly most abstract element of
verse, its music: the short lines, with their dense consonants, im-
pede speech the way turmoil impedes thought. What the poem
does not do is help the reader to decide the rights and wrongs of
the particular political situation that inspired it. The line "dithering, blathering" seems to encapsulate this paradox: almost child-
ishly gratifying to say and hear, it is about being unable to say or
hear anything meaningful or useful.

This ultimate disjunction between beauty and goodness is
why, as Heaney observes, "the true aesthete would perceive himself . . . as a subversive." And Heaney is anything but subversive.
"There's a good deal of humor in me, I hope; and I have a kind
of sardonic attitude to a lot of things," he says. "But for better or
worse, when I sit opposite to the desk, it's like being an altar boy
in the sacristy getting ready to go out on the main altar. There's
a gravitas comes over me."

The allusion to the church of his boyhood is significant.
While Heaney was not an orthodox Catholic, he acknowledged
Catholicism as a continuing influence, above all on his sense of
the value of "passive suffering": "But the idea that your own tra-
vails could earn grace for others, for the souls in purgatory, for

instance, was appealing: my mind worked on those lines all right, my sense that there was value in selfless endurance." At Queen's College, Belfast, Heaney recalled ruefully, "everybody was provided with their own inner priest."

The inner priest survived in Heaney the poet, not in any dogma or doctrine, but in his sense that it is his duty to fortify, to offer consolation. His strongest statement of this principle comes in his essay "Joy or Night," where he considers Philip Larkin's exceedingly unconsoling poem "Aubade": "Being brave / Lets no one off the grave. / Death is no different whined at than withstood." Heaney endorses Miłosz's criticism that Larkin has defaulted on the poet's obligation to be "on the side of life." "Aubade," Heaney writes, "does add weight to the negative side of the scale and tips the balance definitely in favor of chemical law and mortal decline. The poem does not hold the lyre up in the face of the gods of the underworld."

Another way of stating Heaney's objection is that he blames Larkin for telling the plain truth about death, rather than wreathing it in metaphor. But what Larkin says about death and the afterlife in "Aubade" is not substantively different from what Heaney himself says in "Clearances," his sequence about the death of his mother: "The space we stood around had been emptied / Into us to keep." Here, as for Larkin, there is no soul and no afterlife, except in the memory of the survivors. What makes "Clearances" seem like a more affirmative poem than "Aubade" is only the metaphor which turns the absence of an empty space into a presence that can be "emptied into us," the way a wine bottle is emptied by pouring out its contents into a cup.

This is the distinction upon which Heaney insists in "Joy or Night": "In order that human beings bring about the most radiant conditions for themselves to inhabit, it is essential that the vision of reality which poetry offers be transformative, more than just a printout of the given circumstances of its time and place." But this interdict against poetry as "a printout" is, no doubt by design, deeply ambiguous. It can be read aesthetically, as an insistence that the language of poetry be heightened from the language of life—that it possess what Heaney calls "forcibleness," "the attribute that makes you feel the lines have been decreed, that there has been no fussy picking and choosing of words but instead a surge of utterance." But it can also be read ethically, as a warning not to set down the truth if the truth is not conducive to "radiance."

The problem with this second interpretation becomes clear in Heaney's Nobel Lecture, "Crediting Poetry," where he declares:

> Yet there are times when a deeper need enters, when we want the poem to be not only pleasurably right but compellingly wise, not only a surprising variation played upon the world, but a retuning of the world itself. We want the surprise to be transitive, like the impatient thump which unexpectedly restores the picture to the television set, or the electric shock which sets the fibrillating heart back to its proper rhythm. We want what the woman wanted in the prison queue in Leningrad, standing

there blue with cold and whispering for fear, enduring the terror of Stalin's regime and asking the poet Anna Akhmatova if she could describe it all, if her art could be equal to it.

This is a revealingly partial interpretation of the section "Instead of a Preface" that begins Akhmatova's poetic sequence "Requiem." For what the suffering woman demands of the poet, during "the terrible years of the Yezhov terror," is simply "Can you describe this?" And Akhmatova's response is simply "I can." There is nothing "transitive" about this promise, no sense that the poem can cure the mortal ailment it diagnoses. The poem can only tell the truth—or, one might say, offer a "printout" of its horribly wounded "time and place." This is what it means for poetry to be "equal to" evil: not in the sense of an opposing force of equal strength, but in the sense of a candor, a purpose, that does not flinch. Akhmatova describes the stranger's response to her terse affirmative this way: "Then something like a smile passed fleetingly over what had once been her face." It is not unlike the smile that we ourselves might smile when agreeing with Larkin that "death is no different whined at than withstood": the honest but helpless registration of sympathy with a fellow sufferer.

It is very characteristic that Heaney's interpretation of the Akhmatova story rests on this ambiguity in his use of the word "equal." What he intends as a healing reconciliation between the two senses of the word can appear, to a resisting reader, more like an equivocation. At its most extreme, Heaney's desire to "show an affirming flame" leads to writing that he describes, in *Stepping Stones*, as "public in the megaphone sense of the word," like the much-quoted lines from "The Cure at Troy," his translation of Sophocles's *Philoctetes:* "once in a lifetime / The longed-for tidal wave / Of justice can rise up / And hope and history rhyme." This passage was a favorite of Bill Clinton, who alluded to it in the title of his book *Between Hope and History*. Yet Heaney acknowledges that the lines belong "in the realm of pious aspiration."

In his most serious work, however, Heaney is pious in another, more provocative way: he is reverent toward language itself. As he puts it in his Nobel Lecture: "The resolution and independence which the entirely realized poem sponsors . . . has as much to do with the energy released by linguistic fission and fusion, with the buoyancy generated by cadence and tone and rhyme and stanza, as it has to do with the poem's concerns or the poet's truthfulness." Perhaps only a poet whose capacity for pleasure is as great as his sense of responsibility could place such trust in the convertibility of the ethical and the aesthetic. Heaney's greatest power is not to strengthen and console—Larkin, precisely because of his hard lucidity, is a more consoling poet—but to celebrate. This, too, can be a kind of sacred task, but it requires the poet to be less a priest than a mage or a shaman—public figures both, except that they have less regard for their audience than for the spirits of nature that inspire them. It makes sense that Heaney named D. H. Lawrence and Ted Hughes as important early influences, for he shares their rapt attention to things and creatures. His poems often take the form of hymns to the inhuman: "A Bat on the Road," "Badgers," "Mint."

Both Lawrence and Hughes, too, could have written poems titled "The Guttural Muse," as Heaney did. Heaney is capable of many registers—he can be courtly, argumentative, or rhetorical as the occasion demands—but his characteristic style, the one that makes his lines so instantly recognizable, creates a chthonic music out of dense consonants and mouthed vowels: "I love this turf-face, / its black incisions, / the cooped secrets / of process and ritual." A key ingredient in this music is the Ulster dialect, even the local place-names, that Heaney makes use of so often and so unapologetically. O'Driscoll asks Heaney about one such line, "Where kesh and loaning finger out to heather": "Did you expect non-Ulster readers to engage in some research or was it your hope that context and cadence would provide sufficient illumination of the meaning?" To which Heaney gives a refreshingly insouciant answer: "I didn't think at all of the reader's problem when I wrote the line. The joy was in solving my own writer's need."

Heaney, in other words, like all great poets, does not hold himself answerable to the reader in the first instance. He serves the reader, to be sure, but he does so by holding himself responsible to his subjects and his language. This is the process that he describes and enacts in the early poem "Gifts of Rain":

> The tawny guttural water
> spells itself: Moyola
> is its own score and consort,
>
> bedding the locale
> in the utterance,

To make the world spell itself, to turn locale into utterance, is the most fundamental purpose of poetry, and the most joyful. The true significance of Heaney's goodness, it may be, is that by satisfying his conscience, he could shelter the unaccountable space where this transformation happens. He refused to be subversive so that he could permit himself the felicity of the aesthete. Does Heaney not tell us as much in "North"?

> It said, "Lie down
> in the word-hoard, burrow
> the coil and gleam
> of your furrowed brain. . . .
>
> Keep your eye clear
> as the bleb of the icicle,
> trust the feel of what nubbed treasure
> your hands have known."

The Faith of Christian Wiman

Poets often write, or used to, about their longing for posterity. But posterity is faceless, an abstraction, compared with the past, which we can know intimately in the persons of the poets we love. Dante fantasized about meeting Homer, Ovid, and Virgil in the afterlife; Keats mused, "I think I shall be among the English poets after my death." And if poets long for the companionship of the dead, it is because they very often have trouble feeling at home in the company of the living. As Christian Wiman writes in his essay "A Piece of Prose," "poetry arises out of absence, a deep internal sense of wrongness, out of a mind that feels itself to be in some way cracked. An original poem is a descent into and expression of this insufficiency."

Today it is unfashionable to insist that being a poet is a kind of fate, and an ambiguous one at that—a fate that involves separation and suffering as well as lucidity and achievement. For a fate is something given, not chosen; as the Romans said long ago, *poeta nascitur, non fit*, a poet is born, not made. In America today, we tend to take the opposite view. The idea that you have to be born with a gift sounds undemocratic, elitist, contrary to our ideal of openness. Yet Wiman was somehow able to maintain his conviction of the rareness of poetry even while editing *Poetry*. Indeed, he might be the only editor of a poetry magazine brave enough to write that he preferred not to publish too much poetry. "I think a strong case can be made," he once editorialized, "that the more respect you have for poetry, the less of it you will find adequate to your taste and needs. . . . We shouldn't lose sight of one of poetry's chief strengths: how little of it there is."

One sign of a genuine poet is that he is aware of how difficult it is to earn that title. In his first book of prose, *Ambition and Survival*, Wiman writes wryly about his own early poetic aspirations. In his essay "Milton in Guatemala," he recalls, "I was in Guatemala because I thought a writer needed a store of EXPERIENCE, and I was reading Milton because I thought that the only way to write GREAT POEMS, which is all I wanted to do, was to come to terms with the GREAT POEMS of the past. I haven't altogether outgrown those ideas and impulses, though I am less inclined now to go around in my daily life talking in capital letters." He is poking gentle fun at his younger self, but not disavowing him. To this day, while enduring enormous changes in his art and life, Wiman still aims to write great poems. At least, he does write them, and surely it's not possible to write them by accident.

In putting together the words "ambition" and "survival," Wiman suggests an opposition, almost a binary. Writing about his early adulthood, he consistently dwells on the way artistic ambition draws on and produces a sense of alienation from life. In "Milton in Guatemala," Wiman offers a nice metaphor for this alienation in the image of himself as a boarder living in "a tiny box made of corrugated tin and cardboard" on the roof of a family's house: "Through a large hole in the middle of the floor I could see the kitchen," he writes. "It was the hole that caused me some anxiety. When I knew I was going to get drunk . . . I'd set various objects around its edges in the hope that a kicked can or bottle top might clatter down into that underworld before I did." The poet is literally above ordinary life, reduced to spying on it through a hole, afraid of falling calamitously into it. He reminds us of Baudelaire's albatross, who knows how to fly but not how to walk.

Meanwhile, Wiman recalls, he set himself the goal of reading through Milton's complete poems at a rate of fifteen pages a night. And in this essay, his experiences in Guatemala blend with his experience of reading Milton in a way that reveals what it means to think poetically. T. S. Eliot wrote in "The Metaphysical Poets" that "when a poet's mind is perfectly equipped for its work, it is constantly amalgamating disparate experience; the ordinary man's experience is chaotic, irregular, fragmentary. The latter falls in love, or reads Spinoza, and these two experiences have nothing to do with each other, or with the noise of the typewriter or the smell of cooking; in the mind of the poet these experiences are always forming new wholes."

Just so, for Wiman the smell of coffee and avocado, the sight of a religious procession, and overhearing his neighbors making love all combine into a human insight that takes the form of a literary-critical insight about Milton, "a kind of artist who finds that life is most life as it is being obliterated by—or, more accurately, into—art." "There are people of abstract passion," Wiman goes on to observe, "people whose emotional lives are intense but, for one reason or another, interior, their energies accumulating always at the edge of action, either finding no outlet into reality, or ones too small for the force that warps them. This is my sense of Milton." It is also, plainly, the fate that he sees lying in store for himself, and that he both affirms and strives to avoid. If Milton's eloquence is a form of baffled energy, does that mean life must be baffled for art to flourish? Does the life of a serious poet have to be "obliterated"?

For Wiman, prose is a way of working out the same concerns that animate his poetry. "In prose as in poetry, there is perhaps only one definite requirement for a vital style: it must make a reader feel that something is truly at stake," he writes. And in his early poetry, the problem of the incommensurability of art and life comes up again and again. His first two books, *The Long Home* and *Hard Night*, are full of moments when a true, full relation to life, to the world, or to other people suddenly looms up as a possibility, only to vanish just as quickly. Take the poem "Clearing," in which "a green clearing in the trees" becomes an irresistible metaphor:

> you could believe
> that standing in a late weave of light and shade,
> a man could suddenly want his life,
> feel it blaze in him and mean,
> as for a moment I believed,
> before I walked on.

This is a poem about hope that turns out to be profoundly desperate. To actually want your own life is, Wiman suggests, always only the experience of a moment. A clearing is a place where someone on a journey can take a momentary rest, but it's not a home. And Wiman gives no indication that a home can be made in the "blaze" of fulfillment, which, as the word implies, is destined to burn itself out. As he writes in the poem "Elsewhere," "Home / is momentary, a way / of seeing." This experience of homelessness is, in Wiman's case, partly biographical. In several of his early essays, he dwells on how far he traveled from his West Texas childhood, both physically and spiritually. In "On Being Nowhere," the first essay in *Ambition and Survival*, Wiman notes that he moved forty times in fifteen years. He quotes Simone Weil, who is a touchstone in his work: "We must be rooted in the absence of a place. We must take the feeling of being at home into exile."

This feeling of homelessness also marks Wiman's affinity with the Romantic tradition in English poetry. Such poets know that it is hard to be fully at home in this world, that there is something awry in the relationship between man and Being. Exactly how and why this occlusion takes place varies depending on the terms of each poet's metaphor, or myth. The fault can lie with nature or spirit, society or religion, man or God. For the early Romantics, like Wordsworth and Keats, however, there was a remedy, which was poetry itself. Poetry was the language in which the breach between real and ideal could be at once named and closed. In "Tintern Abbey," Wordsworth cherishes

> that blessed mood,
> In which the burthen of the mystery,
> In which the heavy and the weary weight
> Of all this unintelligible world,
> Is lightened:—that serene and blessed mood,
> In which the affections gently lead us on,—
> Until, the breath of this corporeal frame
> And even the motion of our human blood
> Almost suspended, we are laid asleep
> In body, and become a living soul:
> While with an eye made quiet by the power
> Of harmony, and the deep power of joy,
> We see into the life of things.

Wiman finds his clearing, his "momentary" home, in such "blessed" moments. In his early work, however, the poet's hope is usually turned against itself, for it is the condition of being a poet that he holds responsible for the alienation which then becomes the subject of his poetry. In his essay "A Mile from Hell," he speaks of "a wider loss, which I would call consciousness." This is a loss that acts more like a sin, in the sense that it doesn't just happen to us; rather, we choose to inflict it on ourselves. In this sense it is closely allied to pride, which for a certain kind of person is the most dangerous sin, since it turns strength—of will, of mind—into a deadly weakness. Not for nothing is pride the sin that cast Milton's Satan into Hell; and not for nothing was Wiman so drawn to *Paradise Lost*. Milton's Hell is fiery, while Wiman's, in "This Inwardness, This Ice," is frozen and lonely: "Nowhere to go but on, / to creep, and breathe, and learn / a blue beyond belief."

This ice-scape's inwardness is crucial, for the sin of pride isolates, just as the wound of consciousness does. In Wiman's first two books, there is a constant longing to break out of the prison of the self, to join in what looks like the unselfconscious existence of other people. In the title poem of his first book, "The Long Home"—an extended dramatic monologue in which Wiman inhabits the voice of his own grandmother—he tries to imagine the life of those who, as Flaubert put it, are *dans le vrai*, "in the truth." In the lives of his ancestors, Wiman finds the rootedness in nature and family and tradition that he describes as missing not only from his own life, but also from the lives of all the poets he knows. "The Long Home," in addition to being a tour de force of iambic pentameter, is a profound act of familial piety, a way for the wayward poet to write himself back into the place and the people he has left behind. The poem's last scene shows the grandmother leading her grandson around the site where her house used to stand. It is gone now—"My grandson walks through walls he does not see"—but it lives again in his verse and in his memory. Poetry, which alienates the poet from those closest to him, also offers a way back to them.

Still, in Wiman's second book, *Hard Night*, there is an unmistakable disillusion with this kind of abstract, artistic fulfillment. In "Sweet Nothing," whose music is inspired by the densely plainspoken style of Robert Lowell's *Life Studies*, the poet is living in an apartment in San Francisco, where he is able to overhear all the domestic noises made by his upstairs neighbor, an Englishwoman named Rebecca. Inspired by a long walk and conversation with Rebecca, the poet fantasizes about another life, which would be, again, a life healed of self-consciousness:

> One does grow tired,
> tired of pondering
> some problem of balance
> or proportion, wondering
> what's next, what's safe
> to touch; tired
> of coming into rooms
> rain has seeped through,
> the walls awry, the floor
> buckling upward; tired
> of matching grain

to grain, seam to seam,
to make some one thing
that will not, one knows,
in time, remain.

The "rooms" that Wiman writes about are actually stanzas
—the word means "room" in Italian—and the finicky labor of
"matching grain to grain, seam to seam" is his metaphor for the
ungrateful work of writing poetry. The ambitious poet is in-
fected by what Philip Larkin ruefully called "arrogant eternity,"
the idea that writing is an avenue to immortality. Wiman, typically, feels the tug of this ambition while also recognizing it as
an illusion, since no poem will endure forever. Wouldn't it be
better, instead of constantly being thrown into the future, to
cherish the present, with its sights and sensations? And couldn't
love be the key to this kind of wholeness? But the poem ends on
an irresolute note, with the poet merely dreaming of the woman
he does not actually possess, just as he doesn't possess the ability
to "drift through the days."

The self-dissatisfaction threaded through *Hard Night* culmi-
nates in "Being Serious," a bleakly hilarious sequence of poems
about a man who is named, and is, Serious. Like John Berryman's
Henry, Serious is Wiman's exaggerated alter ego, and we follow
him from the moment of birth to the moment of death. Since
Wiman himself is nothing if not serious, Serious becomes a way
for the poet to reflect on the aspects of his character that he finds
burdensome, even absurd. For instance, Serious—who has en-

counters with other people named Stupid, Timid, and Mad—is clearly an intellectual: "Serious sits through opera without a yawn, / Chews up books on which weaker teeth would shatter . . . / Serious knows some things."

But Serious, for all his knowledge, is never happy. The moment he is born, his first thought is "I'm fucked." As an adult, he marries, then divorces, and is always haunted by the same sense of loneliness and insufficiency. In "Serious gives a speech," he proclaims that "To be serious is to be alone!" and explains in a way that resonates with many moments in Wiman's poetry:

> To be serious, to be truly serious, is to know
> That what you call your losses you cannot grieve,
> For it was never quite these things that you wanted
> —This treasure, this touch, this one place—
> But by such life to be haunted.

Here is the predicament of the poet, who does not want to live, but to stand at what Wiman elsewhere calls "a strange adjacency to experience," in order to see it and write about it. But such a position comes at a cost: when it turns out that Serious is orating to an empty auditorium, the poem's scenario reveals itself as a nightmare. The isolation that the poet craves, even boasts about, returns with a vengeance when it turns out that no one is interested in his problems. His despair threatens to become the sole subject of his art, or of any art, as he reflects: "an art that's truly great / Will always have one deepest truth to tell, / which is, my friend, this life is hell." Wiman is thinking of Milton's Satan, who said, "Which way I fly is Hell; myself am Hell; / And, in the lowest deep, a lower deep / Still threatening to devour me opens wide, / To which the Hell I suffer seems a Heaven." This is the Hell of solipsism, which every person potentially carries in his own mind, and which Serious falls into precisely because of his pride in being so serious.

This is the situation, the dead end, one might say, where we leave Wiman at the end of his second book, which was published in 2005. When we meet him again in *Every Riven Thing*, published five years later, it is immediately clear that there has been a revolution in his life and in his poetry: he has fallen sick with a rare and incurable form of cancer, and fallen in love with a woman who became his wife. Wiman is not a confessional poet—he lacks the relish in self-exposure, the Freudian zest, that you find in poets like Lowell and Berryman. Despite this modesty, however, the truth is that few contemporary poets put their own actual experience into their work in such a compelling manner as Wiman. There is nothing easier for a poet than to write about him- or herself; the art lies in making that self representative, in turning one's own experience into a metaphor or an allegory in which the reader, too, can see his reflection. To be able to do this requires a self-knowledge and a generosity that are moral qualities as much as aesthetic ones.

Such magnanimity can be found in Wiman's essay "Love Bade Me Welcome," whose title is taken from George Herbert. Here

Wiman communicates the rupture in his life and writing whose repercussions will be felt in all his subsequent work. He begins by saying that at some point he stopped writing poetry—a silence that makes sense coming after *Hard Night*, with its persistent awareness of poetry as a trap. Then came the rapture of falling in love, followed immediately by the devastation of a cancer diagnosis. And under the pressure of these experiences, Wiman finds himself thinking about God in a new way. He returns to a double-edged saying of Simone Weil's: "It is necessary to have had a revelation of reality through joy in order to find reality through suffering." Wiman goes on to write:

> This is certainly true to my own experience. I was not wrong all those years to believe that suffering is at the very center of our existence, and that there can be no untranquilized life that does not fully confront this fact. The mistake lay in thinking grief the means of confrontation, rather than love. To come to this realization is not to be suddenly "at ease in the world." I don't really think it's possible for humans to be at the same time conscious and comfortable.

What has changed, in Wiman's work—what perhaps always changes in what we call a conversion—is not the content of experience, but the perspective on it. Fleeting moments of grace had always appeared in his poetry, but previously his emphasis was on their disappearance, their refusal to stay and last. Now there is a determination to find the truth of the world in grace's arrival, rather than its departure.

This involves Wiman in a paradoxical kind of faith, which he explores in his prose book *My Bright Abyss*. His language is Christian: that is the religion in which he was raised, and to which he returned after a long absence. But he also insists on a distinction between faith and belief: "Faith is nothing more—but how much this is—than a motion of the soul toward God," he writes. "It is not belief. Belief has objects—Christ was resurrected, God created the earth—faith does not." Christianity is such a long tradition that different poets can find very different resources in it. When George Herbert addresses God, in "The Call," he does so in terms of love and intimacy:

> Come, my Joy, my Love, my Heart:
> Such a Joy, as none can move:
> Such a Love, as none can part:
> Such a Heart, as joyes in love.

John Donne, on the other hand, summons God in his "Holy Sonnets" in the language of terror and exhilaration:

> Batter my heart, three-person'd God; for you
> As yet but knock, breathe, shine, and seek to mend;
> That I may rise, and stand, o'erthrow me and bend
> Your force, to break, blow, burn, and make me new.

Gerard Manley Hopkins sees God in the flashing inscape of things. T. S. Eliot, who wrote only half ironically that "the spirit killeth, the letter giveth life," sees Christianity as a source of cosmic, social, and personal order.

For Wiman, who carries on this tradition in a time when explicitly religious verse has grown rare, the Christian concept that seems most urgent is the incarnation, the idea that God chose to inhabit this life alongside us. "Christ is contingency," he writes, and it is the penetration of this fallen world by God that is the ultimate mystery, and the key to redemption. In the sequence "More Like the Stars," from *Once in the West*, Wiman writes of "the love that from beyond being / has come to us: / / Christ's ever unhearable / and thus always too bearable / scream."

Because God is unhearable much of the time, we must cultivate stillness if we are to be attuned to him. "A god, if it's a living one, is not outside of reality but in it, of it, though in ways it takes patience and imagination to perceive," Wiman writes. In this way, his adult faith differs profoundly from the faith of his childhood: "I was brought up with the poisonous notion that you had to renounce love of the earth in order to receive the love of God. My experience has been just the opposite: a love of the earth and existence so overflowing that it implied, or included, or even absolutely demanded, God. Love did not deliver me from the earth, but into it." This is the theme of the title poem of *Every Riven Thing*:

> God goes, belonging to every riven thing he's made
> sing his being simply by being
> the thing it is:
> stone and tree and sky,
> man who sees and sings and wonders why . . .

Each of the poem's stanzas begins with the same line, but Wiman varies the punctuation, and therefore the meaning. Should we say "God goes belonging," present in everything? Or is it that "God goes," absent from everything? Could these two states coexist, like the quantum states of an electron, so that they finally come to mean the same thing? In all its versions, the word that stands out in the line is "riven": a forceful, antique word, meaning torn or split apart. It is not the whole things where we find God, but the broken ones—a belief central to Christianity, whose central symbol is the cross, which was an instrument for breaking the human body.

Under this sign, Wiman writes with unremitting intensity about the quest for grace in a world full of pain and humiliation. His language is more innovative than ever before, while also moving toward a restraint that takes the form of letting things be themselves. Like Frost, he begins to write poems in which things become their own metaphors, without needing to be spelled out; the world interprets itself. "It Takes Particular Clicks" is about something as quotidian as walking a dog; Wiman contrasts the kind of knowledge that was characteristic of Serious—knowledge of the whole—with the animal knowledge of his dog, for whom the important things are the particularities. Meaning is not found by putting everything together in an act of poetic synthesis; that way lies pride, and aridity, and solipsism. Rather, meaning emerges clandestinely, and the only way to capture it is by staying quietly alert. Here again Wiman seems to converge with Wordsworth, whose watchword was "wise passiveness."

One difference between Wiman and Wordsworth is that the latter was content to call the thing we seek Nature, while for Wiman it is definitely God. It would be a mistake to pass too quickly over this distinction, to reduce it merely to a metaphor. Nature is easier of approach than God, who is both in and out of Nature. In "Given a God More Playful," Wiman almost wishes for a Wordsworthian relationship with Nature: "Given a god more playful . . . / I might have swigged existence / from a tulip's bell." But there is no dancing like the daffodils for this poet, who remains too much like Serious to dance. Indeed, his world offers few flowers: the landscapes of his poetry, whether the mesquite trees of Texas or the steel girders of the El in Chicago, tend to be harsh and ungiving. The experience of sickness has shown him the worst face of Nature, the face that speaks of pain and decay and death. And as his sense of the truth has changed, so too has his motive for metaphor, his sense of why it is poets write in the first place. The young Wiman spoke of the highest kind of artistic ambition, rare and honorable, which Milton called "the last infirmity of noble mind." In his later work, this infirmity seems left behind, in favor of a deeper kind of generosity. As he writes in *My Bright Abyss:*

> In truth, experience means nothing if it does not mean beyond itself: we mean nothing unless and until our hard-won mean-

ings are internalized and catalyzed within the lives of others. There is something I am meant to see, something for which my own situation and suffering are the lens, but the cost of such seeing—I am just beginning to realize—may very well be any final clarity or perspective on my own life, my own faith. That would not be a bad fate, to burn up like the booster engine that falls away from the throttling rocket, lighting a little dark as I go.

Posterity remains on Wiman's mind, but now it is not an audience to impress. It is more like a family of descendants, for whom he wants to play the same comforting and strengthening role that his own ancestors did for him. And the generosity of this ambition has been rewarded in a fitting way: for it is vanishingly rare for any poet to reach so many people, so deeply, as Wiman does. Writing in the dark, he has lit the way for thousands of readers.

Kay Ryan: The Less Deceived

Kay Ryan became a famous poet in much the same way Ernest Hemingway described going broke: gradually and then suddenly. She was nearing forty when her first, self-published book appeared, in 1983, but neither that debut nor the two books that followed got much response from readers or critics. In 1999, when Dana Gioia wrote an essay calling attention to Ryan's work, it was the first substantial review she had received. Gioia recalled that he had discovered Ryan "almost by accident," when he was given a copy of her 1994 collection *Flamingo Watching*. "No critical fanfare accompanied the slender volume," he wrote, "and I had no special reason to think it possessed singular merit." Though Ryan was then forty-four, and had been publishing for the better part of two decades, Gioia still considered her a "new" poet.

Just over a decade later, Ryan was named poet laureate of the

United States and won the Pulitzer Prize. Yet to speak of her success in conventional career terms, however accurate it may be, feels like an irrelevance, if not an impertinence. "One can't work / by limelight," Ryan wrote in a punning poem in her 2000 collection, *Say Uncle:* "A bowlful / right at / one's elbow / produces no / more than / a baleful / glow against / the kitchen table." Certainly, her increasing prominence did not make her any less cutting about the poetry world that sought to honor her. In a wonderfully impolite essay published in *Poetry* in 2005, she wrote about attending the annual convention of Associated Writing Programs, the umbrella organization for all the nation's university creative-writing departments. Ryan compared the event, with its 230-page schedule and its fifteen simultaneous panels, to a trip to Costco: "The AWP catalog says to you, as the Costco shopping cart says to you, Think big! Glut yourself!"

To a poet like Ryan, nothing could be more anathema than bigness. Open her collected poems, *The Best of It*, to any page, and you will find a narrow column of verse, held aloft by taut rhythms and irregular rhymes. Her poems are seldom longer than a page, and never longer than two. There have been great poets devoted to glut, but Ryan belongs to the other, usually more trustworthy camp, the one ruled by what she calls "That Will to Divest." In American poetry, the contest between glut and divestment is inevitably epitomized by Whitman and Dickinson. Between these two tutelary spirits, Ryan would of course choose Dickinson, and the resemblances between them have been made much of by critics. This is natural—after all, Ryan, too, writes brief, compressed lyrics, and has been a kind of outsider to the literary world. But the comparison does not really capture Ryan's style and personality, and she sometimes seems to be consciously repudiating it, as in the poem "Hope." Hope, to Dickinson, is the thing with feathers that perches in the soul; to Ryan, it is merely "the almost-twin / of making-do, / the isotope / of going on." The chemical vocabulary dissents from Dickinson's imagery, just as Ryan's wry pessimism keeps its distance from Dickinson's metaphysical despair.

Often, in fact, the poet Ryan sounds most like is Philip Larkin. She, too, aspires to be one of "The Less Deceived," to use the title of Larkin's second book. Certainly Larkin would have appreciated the metaphor in "The Niagara River," the title poem of Ryan's 2005 collection. "We / do know, we do / know this is the / Niagara River, but / it is hard to remember / what that means," she writes, and her deliberate refusal to name the famous falls in the poem both mirrors and mocks our tendency to ignore the ending we are all heading for. Larkin was another sharp critic of the poetry world; he was in the university, but as a librarian he was not quite of it, just as Ryan has been a professor not of creative writing but of remedial English, at a community college in Marin County.

Perhaps because she grew up in remote parts of California— the San Joaquin Valley and the Mojave Desert, far from the coastal metropolises—Ryan has a pronounced sympathy with those who approach poetry with a sense that they are entering a foreign country. One early poem, "A Certain Meanness of Culture"—the phrase is T. S. Eliot's dismissive description of William Blake— proclaims her allegiance to those "born on deserts" who "start to value culture / like you would water." "You get pretty stringy and impatient / with the fat smoke off / old cities," she writes, sounding like a New World populist in the William Carlos Williams tradition.

But this persona is not a good fit for Ryan, whose poems feature epigrams from and references to Fernando Pessoa, Martin Buber, and Joseph Brodsky (as well as "Ripley's Believe It or Not!"). Rather, she is a democratic elitist, believing that many are called but few are chosen. It is precisely because she earned her own intimate relationship with literature—because she needs "culture / like you would water"—that she believes in greatness, which is simply another name for effectiveness: great writing is writing that really does quench your thirst. She has no patience for the clumsy sincerity of what she calls, in one poem, "Outsider Art": "There never / seems to be a surface equal / to the needs of these people. . . . / We are not / pleased the way we thought / we would be pleased."

Indeed, Ryan dares to sound the unfashionable note of high poetic ambition: "Few are / the willing / and fewer / the champions," she writes in "Repetition." This kind of ambition would be familiar to Whitman and Dickinson, but it is another barrier between Ryan and the poetry world. In her essay in *Poetry*, she describes listening to panelists talk about how teaching creative writing fuels their own creativity, and feeling the same kind of guilt a four-star chef might feel at a church potluck: "My sense of this panel, mostly made up of women and attended by women for what reason I can't say, is that these are sincere, helpful, useful people who show their students their own gifts and help them to enjoy the riches of language while also trying to get some writing done themselves. They have to juggle these competing demands upon their souls and it is hard and honorable. I agree and shoot me now."

This is abrasive, and so, at its best, is Ryan's poetry, as in "Periphery": "Fountains, for instance, / have a periphery / at some distance / from the spray. / On nice days / idle people circle / all the way around / the central spout. / They do not get wet. / They do not get hot." It is Ryan's version of Frost's complaint: "They cannot look out far. / They cannot look in deep." Reading her, one remembers that abrasiveness used to be a prized characteristic of American literature, a reflection of the democratic orneriness of the homesteader and the frontiersman. Now that literature is largely a profession and an institution, it is hard to imagine how D. H. Lawrence could ever have said that "the essential American soul is hard, isolate, stoic, and a killer."

Ryan is no killer, of course, though when she writes about nature she does tend to sympathize more with the predator than with the prey: "Rabbits are one of the things / coyotes are for," she observes. But Lawrence's other adjectives are a faithful enough description. "It takes a courageous / person to leave spaces / empty," Ryan writes in "Leaving Spaces," condemning the medieval mapmakers who filled up their blanks with monsters or pretty designs: "Of course they were cowards / and patronized by cowards." She uses the same metaphor when protesting creative-writing classes: "One must truly HOLD A SPACE for oneself. All things conspire to close up this space."

If this were simply a complaint about the poetry world, it could be dismissed as mere crankiness; as an expression of Ryan's sensibility, or even her philosophy of life, it goes much deeper. It may seem like a paradox that a poet who makes so much of her independence should turn out to be one of the best contemporary poets of marriage. But it is precisely because Ryan values true companionship so highly that she scorns its easy simulacra. In interviews, Ryan has spoken about the role that her wife, Carol Adair, played in her development as a writer; in a profile, she called Adair "my strongest advocate and my single companion in my poetry life." Yet aside from the dedication—"For Carol / who knew it"—Adair's name never appears in *The Best of It.*

This reticence is entirely in keeping with Ryan's approach to poetry, which developed in reaction to the vogue for confessional poetry in the 1960s. "I just didn't like the style that saying 'poet' meant," Ryan said. "Anne Sexton was a poet. Robert Lowell was a poet. People who cut a dramatic swath. Lots of medication. I didn't want to be dramatic." When Lowell wrote about his marital griefs, he spared no details: "Why not say what happened?" he asks in a late poem. With Ryan, by contrast, it is entirely possible to read her 1996 collection, *Elephant Rocks*, without fully realizing that she is chronicling a domestic crisis. It becomes clear only in retrospect, for instance, that "Hope," that despairing poem—which speaks of "the always tabled / righting of the present"—is part of the same sequence that includes "Bad Patch," "Swept Up Whole," and "Relief," each observing a moment in the trajectory of a marriage or love affair. In fact, the more directly Ryan writes about desire, the more indirect she becomes, as befits a poet for whom, it seems, the most important things are the ones that are hardest to say. In "Green Hills," for instance, is Ryan writing about landscape, or about young, unattainable bodies, or both, when she observes, "Their green flanks / and swells are not / flesh in any sense / matching ours, / we tell ourselves"?

Certainly it is not just the fish we are supposed to sympathize with in "To the Young Anglerfish," when Ryan, spurred by a quotation from Stephen Jay Gould, sympathizes with a creature caught in mid-evolution, its lower nature at war with its higher one: "Meanwhile, the problems of life enhance: / an awkwardness attends the mating dance / and an inexplicable thoughtfulness / at the wrong moments." Here it is easy to recognize the classic complaint of the writer (usually, however, the young writer) who finds self-consciousness inhibiting instinct, especially when it comes to sex. The problem is that self-consciousness, "inexplicable thoughtfulness," is also the writer's greatest point of pride.

It is what makes Ryan, in the title of another poem, "Cut Out for It": "Cut out / as a horse / is cut / from the / pack," she finds her very isolation is what gives her "such a feeling / for the way / they touch / and shift / as one, the / beauty when / they run."

This melancholy lucidity is Ryan's greatest gift. But her most startling discovery is that melancholy, with its tendency to brood and spread, is best contained in a form that is tight, witty, almost sprightly sounding. Her poems are often built on the logic of the pun, taking an ordinary word or dead cliché as a title and then jolting it to unexpected life. In "Bitter Pill," Ryan makes the title phrase surprisingly literal: it is an actual pill, in a bottle with "your name" on it, and the bitterness is not just that of seeing a loved one sick but of actually swallowing the medicine. In "Dogleg," Ryan first challenges the title word by observing that "only two of / the dog's legs / dogleg," then extends its meaning by seeing it as an emblem of those moments "when life has / angled brutally."

But the pun is not a very challenging kind of wit, and Ryan's least satisfying poems are those in which she settles for the easy payoff of verbal comedy. "Bestiary," for instance, begins, "A bestiary catalogs / bests," and goes on to contrast it with a "goodiary." "Extraordinary Lengths" imagines "lengths / swagged from balconies, / ribbons of lengths rippling," and so on. Where Ryan's technique truly justifies itself is when pun deepens into symbol. In "Chop," Ryan turns the footprint of a bird on the beach into an "emperor's chop"—that is, a Chinese stamp or seal, used for signing documents. But the point of the poem is what happens to that proud signature: "Stride, stride, / goes the emperor / down his wide / mirrored promenade / the sea bows / to repolish."

The sea seems to be doing homage to the bird-emperor, but in fact it is effacing every trace of his passage—just as, Ryan does not have to say, time and nature do to all our imperial ambitions. A poem like this helps to explain why Ryan would choose to write an elegy for the German writer W. G. Sebald, with whom she seems to have little in common, at least on the surface. But, after all, Sebald wrote a book called *The Rings of Saturn*, and Ryan is another disciple of the god of melancholy. Sebald was obsessed with transience and decay, and Ryan can never stop noticing what she calls, in "Slant," "a bias cut to everything, / a certain cant / it's better not to name." Ryan's poem for Sebald is titled "He Lit a Fire with Icicles," which is both an incident in the life of St. Sebolt, the writer's namesake, and a description of his technique: "How / cold he had / to get to learn / that ice would / burn. How cold / he had to stay," Ryan writes. Her admiration is unmistakable.

Extension of the Domain of Struggle

In 2008, a young novelist named Keith Gessen published his first book, *All the Sad Young Literary Men*. Like many debut novels, it was highly autobiographical; the novelist's own ambition was the book's major theme, and its publication consummated the drive for recognition that was both its inspiration and its subject. Because of this self-reflexive quality, the book took on a symbolic significance. It was a distillation of the kind of literary ambition that consists of wanting to be known as a writer.

This ambition helped to determine the way Gessen's book was received, not so much in the print reviews as on the internet, where it became the target of extraordinarily virulent attacks. Attacks, not criticism—for in the discussion of *All the Sad Young Literary Men*, literary criticism in the ordinary sense played almost no role. Its detractors had little to say about its plot, characters, or prose style. More curiously, perhaps, neither did Gessen, when he took to the internet to defend himself. Both writer and readers treated the book as an assertion of self, and the only question was whether that assertion ought to succeed—whether Gessen ought to become famous. Because this debate was not tethered to something relatively objective, like the book's artistic quality, it had to become at once personal and abstract. The author claimed recognition, the critics wanted to deny it—it was as simple and passionate as that. Inadvertently, they had exposed literature for what at bottom it really is: a power struggle.

According to Hegel, "Self-consciousness exists . . . in that, and by the fact that it exists for another self-consciousness; that is to say, it is only by being acknowledged or 'recognized.'" The infant wants only this, the king and the millionaire take roundabout paths to achieve it, but the writer alone seems able to obtain it immediately. Writers write in order to be recognized. To be recognized as good writers, yes—but that is not enough of a goal to explain the frenzy of literary competition. If writing were simply a skill, demonstrating that one possessed the skill, even in supreme measure, would be as technical and trivial an achievement as something in athletics. It is because writing is a communication of consciousness that it promises to gratify the original desire of spirit: to have one's being confirmed by having it acknowledged by others. Writing makes others the mirror of the self.

But this promise of literature is a strange one. Why, after all, should writing well, an aesthetic achievement, be the price of being recognized, a universal human need? Why shouldn't a writer who simply expresses that need as clearly and urgently as possible be rewarded with the recognition he demands, regardless of whether he has created a beautiful linguistic object? Isn't there something trivial, even monstrous, about a system that makes artistic gifts, which are randomly, amorally distributed, the only means by which recognition can be purchased?

The economic metaphor is not accidental. As far back as we can see, the economics of literary fame have been based on scarcity. There is not enough recognition to go around, so every human being's just claim cannot be met. Beauty is the currency, as arbitrary as gold or paper, in which recognition is bought and sold. We grant great writers the dignity of having really *been*, the posthumous recognition that we call immortality, because they please us with their arrangements of words. Because of how well they wrote, we remember not just their works but their letters, travels, illnesses, aspirations; we feel with and for them. But we do this as irrationally as the peahen decides to mate with the peacock who has the biggest tail feathers, which have nothing intrinsically to do with reproductive fitness.

If the scarcity of recognition is a symptom of the world's fallenness, then literary ambition is a form of complicity with fallenness. In other words, it is a sin. Because there is not enough money in the world, people steal; because there is not enough power, people do violence; because there is not enough recognition, they make art.

The internet, we have heard again and again, is going to transform the future of reading and writing, the way Gutenberg did. Gessen's case, however, suggests that the transformation is not going to be a benign one. Michel Houellebecq titled one of his novels *Extension of the Domain of Struggle* (it was translated into English under the title *Whatever*), and portrayed post-1960s Europe as a place where the competitive principles of capitalism had been extended to sexuality, with disastrous results. In the same way, the internet brings the atomized, absolute competitiveness of capitalism to the struggle for recognition that is literature. Online, there are no mediating institutions—no editors, magazines, publishing houses, or critics—with the power to confer or protect literary reputation.

This ought to be a paradise: a Rousseauan state of nature, uncorrupted by authority and custom, where all readers and writers are free and equal. But it has turned out to be more like a Hobbesian state of nature, where everyone is at war against everyone else. Just look at the way Gessen's readers addressed him online: "The problem with American literature today is you"; "some overrated pretentious writer whose books will end up in the bargain bin at Costco"; "like one of those unbearable leg cramps you get in the middle of the night. Once it's over you kind of want it back just to see if it really was as bad as you remember." Still, there was no ignoring the fact that, for all the abuse he took, Gessen was always attacked by name, while for all their fury, the commenters were always known by their handles. This was an uprising of the have-nots against a have, and like most such uprisings, it could be only a riot, not a revolution. When the dust settles, the published writer is still recognized and his detractors are still anonymous.

The internet has democratized the means of self-expression, but it has not democratized the rewards of self-expression. Now everyone can assert a claim to recognition in a blog, tweet, or Facebook post. But the amount of recognition available in the world is inexorably shrinking, since each passing generation leaves behind more writers with a claim on our memory; that is why the fight for recognition is so fierce and so personal. Yet the trolls who were so indignant at Gessen's attempt to engross more than his share of recognition did not direct their indignation at literature itself. They did not want to end the economy of scarcity, but to move individually from the camp of the have-nots to the camp of the haves. In this they were like the snobbish narrator in Proust, whose fascination with aristocratic titles reached its height just at the historical moment when titles became completely meaningless. They were not revolutionaries but social climbers.

If that is the case, then the best strategy for writers in the age of the internet may be to ignore the internet and look down on it. If print is a luxury, make it a rare and exclusive one. If literature is anti-democratic, revel in its injustice. Make sure that the reward of recognition goes to the most beautiful and difficult writing, not to the loudest and neediest. Above all, do not start tweeting, for the trolls will only despise you for choosing to meet them on their own ground.

People who are reconciled to the injustice of this world console themselves by dreaming of another. It used to be that the poor could look forward to the Kingdom of Heaven. So, too, those who go unrecognized in this world could at least be sure that they were recorded in the Book of Life, where no name was omitted. As Tennyson put it, already in the optative mood: "That nothing walks with aimless feet; / That not one life shall be destroy'd, / Or cast as rubbish to the void, / When God hath made the pile complete."

People who are not reconciled to the injustice of this world, but also don't believe in the justice of the next, take refuge in the imagination of redemption, which is always hypothetical. Their patron saint is Doctor Astrov, the worn-out idealist in Chekhov's *Uncle Vanya*, who retains a glimmer of hope in the future: "You know, when you walk through a forest on a dark night and you see a small light gleaming in the distance, you don't notice your tiredness, nor the darkness, nor the prickly branches lashing you in the face," he explains.

But even Astrov doubts if the millennium will bring him what he, like everyone, most desires: recognition. "I wondered whether the people who come after us in a hundred years' time, the people for whom we are now blasting a trail—would they remember us and speak kindly of us? No, Nanny, I'll wager they won't!" To which the pious old nurse replies, "If people won't remember, God will." Can we, then, bridge the gulf between the actual future, where nobody except a few great men and women will be remembered (if even them), and the ideal future, where everybody is remembered the way they need and deserve?

Imagine it this way. The internet, which seems so sophisticated to us, turns out to be just the first primitive stage in the evolution of a global, networked mind. In time—a thousand years or a million, it doesn't matter—what was once humanity becomes a virtual entity, inhabiting every place and no place, singular and plural at once. These contradictions are simply a way of saying that we can't imagine what it will be like, just as mystics used to define God negatively for want of any real knowledge.

Nor will that future mass-mind be able to imagine what we are like. It will be as divorced from its past as we are from *Homo erectus*, and it will pursue the mystery of its origins as avidly as we theorize about the lightning strike that brought amino acids out of the primordial soup. But one day, on an unfathomably antique level of its memory archive, the mass-mind will unearth the archaic structures that make up our internet. It will decipher these traces of its own past as eagerly as our scholars go to work on Greek papyri recycled as mummy wrappings.

Our scholars, when they decipher old texts, are less delighted when they find yet another copy of Homer or the Bible than when they stumble across the provision lists of a Sumerian king, or the private letters of a Roman legionary posted at Hadrian's Wall. Literature tells us how people thought they were and how they wanted to be seen; but these random, personal, undeliberated traces of ancient lives show us the way they really were. Evidence, not eloquence, is what we need to understand our origins.

So, too, with the virtual mind of the inconceivable future. When it looks for traces of us, it will turn not to novels or poems, but to emails and Facebook pages. Mind will treasure these evidences of its own past and devote all its infinite resources to interpreting them. And because it is infinite, it will have more than enough attention to give to each of our lives. Even the least articulate of us will become the focus of a kind of ancestor cult, subject to the devoted meditation of innumerable intelligences. The first will be made last, and the last first. The scarcity of recognition will give way to the plenitude that has always been the mark of the messianic age. If only we could be certain that this was the future we had in store, no poet would ever have to write another line.

The Poetry of World
and the Poetry of Earth

Contemporary poetry is not often religious, but it is still intensely, covertly metaphysical. Human nature, it seems, compels us to keep asking about the first things, even if we no longer accept the same answers that our ancestors did, or even the same kind of answers. Indeed, it's possible to find in our poetry a distinctive metaphysics that will give our period a retrospective unity, when readers of the future come to survey what looks to us like chaos. And the best document of that sensibility—the single piece of writing that does the most to explain what our poetry believes, and the ways it expresses that belief—is Martin Heidegger's essay "The Origin of the Work of Art."

It is not surprising that poets should continue to turn to Heidegger for inspiration and guidance, since he himself looked to poetry as a model of what thinking should be. Heidegger used individual poems, especially the hymns of Friedrich Hölderlin, to explicate his own ideas about nature, technology, art, and history. He constantly dwelled on the mysteries of language and translation, how the way we name things can reveal and conceal their essence. And he approached writing in a poetic spirit; he uses nouns as verbs and verbs as nouns, puns on etymologies, and even plays with spelling, all in an effort to jar the reader out of conventional ways of reading and thinking.

In "The Origin of the Work of Art," Heidegger issues a particular invitation to poets, arguing that poetry is in some way the model for all other art forms—more, that it is the exemplary activity of human beings. The poet, he writes, "uses the word—not, however, like ordinary speakers and writers who have to use them up, but rather in such a way that the word only now becomes and remains truly a word." Like Ralph Waldo Emerson, Heidegger regards poetry as the truest form of language, and most language as merely defective poetry. "The nature of poetry," he declares, "is the founding of truth."

To explain this numinous formula, Heidegger begins by setting the reader before a particular artwork, a Van Gogh painting of a pair of shoes. When you wear shoes, he points out, you seldom think about them. Shoes, like all kinds of tools and equipment, are at their best when they are most reliable—that is, when they perform their function silently and unobtrusively. You only begin to pay attention to your shoes when they stop working properly, when they pinch your foot or when the sole comes off.

And most of the objects that surround us share this quality of being instruments, things that we use and ignore.

Looking at Van Gogh's painting of a pair of shoes, Heidegger suggests, something different happens. For the first time, we become aware of the two dimensions in which a pair of shoes exists. On the one hand, we are struck by their physical reality: their weight and texture and color, all the qualities we tend to overlook when we wear them. At the same time, the painting allows us to imagine the life in which these shoes belong—the life of a peasant woman, Heidegger imagines, with her "toilsome tread." Crucially, these two aspects of the shoes—what they are and what they do—are inextricable in the painting. "In the stiffly rugged heaviness of the shoes," Heidegger writes, "there is the accumulated tenacity of her slow trudge through the far-spreading and ever-uniform furrows of the field swept by a raw wind. On the leather lie the dampness and richness of the soil. Under the soles slides the loneliness of the field-path as evening falls."

In this way, the philosopher suggests, the Van Gogh painting demonstrates the double purpose of art. Art confronts us with "the earth," the sensuous reality of the nonhuman, which we tend to forget or ignore when we are engaged in practical tasks. At the same time, art sets the earth into "the world," the historical, human context in which we work, suffer, and hope. Artworks can perform this unique function because they themselves have a double nature. They cannot exist without matter, and they always have physical properties—music is formed sound, painting is formed color. But they also do not exist simply in matter, the way utilitarian objects do. Rather, they simultaneously transcend their material and allow their material to be itself for the first time. When we look at a Greek temple, Heidegger writes, we understand the weight and color of marble, in a way that we can't when we're just looking at a rock quarry.

Heidegger dwells on two examples of artworks, the Van Gogh painting and the Greek temple, neither of which are poems. And the dichotomy of earth and world, which seems to suit painting and architecture very well, is hard to apply to poetry, whose material, language, is quite intangible. Yet he continues to insist that poetry "has a privileged position in the domain of the arts." Indeed, Heidegger's description of the worn-out shoes is itself a kind of poem, inspired by Van Gogh's painting but going beyond its source in its evocation of a peasant woman's life. Only the art of language makes possible a full understanding of an artwork's "world." Language, the distinctively human possession, is what allows "stone, plant, and animal" to be fully perceived, in a way that they can't perceive themselves. "Where there is no language ... there is also no openness of what is," Heidegger writes. "Language, by naming beings for the first time, first brings beings to word and to appearance." Only by talking and writing about something can we really understand what it is and what it means.

But just as Heidegger insists that the artwork has a double existence as both earth and world, so his own theory of poetry cuts two ways. If the poet is primarily concerned with earth—with displaying particular being and concrete reality—he will tend to conceive of poetry as a passive art, concerned with perception and preservation. The ideal of such poetry is naming. By finding the right name for every being, the poet functions as Adam did in the Garden of Eden, completing God's creation by bringing it into the human realm of language. But a language is not a language if it is spoken by only one person, and the poet can create names only if they are conveyed to readers and embraced by them. As a result, he stands in a particularly intimate relationship to the reader, whom he regards as a partner in the creation of the work. "Preserving the work," as Heidegger writes, "does not reduce people to their private experiences, but brings them into affiliation with the truth happening in the work."

If, on the other hand, the poet is more concerned with world—with the historical and metaphysical context that the poem creates or invokes—he will tend to see poetry as an active art, and in some sense even a domineering one. The poet of world doesn't just want to preserve an experience with the reader, but to interpret experience for the reader. He goes beyond names to commandments. And Heidegger has a definite sympathy with this kind of poet, as we can see from the way he himself makes a poem out of his description of a Greek temple: "The temple, in its standing there, first gives to things their look and to men their outlook on themselves. This view remains open as long as the work is a work, as long as the god has not fled from it."

Such a temple, with its law-giving god, imposes an order on the world, like Wallace Stevens's jar in Tennessee. But that order, Heidegger reveals in spite of himself, can have sinister implications. The world created by such an artwork may depend on violence; just think of the world of the *Iliad*, full of temples and murders. It may command its inhabitants to make war in pursuit of their destiny. As Heidegger writes, such a work "puts up for decision what is holy and what unholy, what great and what small, what brave and what cowardly, what lofty and what flighty, what master and what slave." He is quoting Heraclitus in that sentence, but the words unmistakably echo the rhetoric of the Third Reich, which was similarly obsessed with greatness and mastery. World-creating art, Heidegger writes, can only belong to a "historical people"—a phrase full of menace for peoples who are "unhistorical," and thus can be eliminated from history.

The story of poetry in the twentieth century could be written in Heideggerian terms, as a turn from the poetry of world to the poetry of earth. The modernists—and Heidegger belonged to the generation of Eliot and Pound—looked to poetry to reestablish a world, at a time when the world they inherited had been shattered. Modernist poetry wanted to serve the same function as a Greek temple, projecting new coordinates of meaning and order. In Yeats's ghosts and gyres, in Pound's sages and tyrants, in Eliot's "idea of a Christian society," we find various attempts to create a world. Yet none of these worlds is authoritative enough to do what the temple did, to inaugurate a new history. Instead, they remain—like Heidegger's own work, perhaps—expressions of longing for a lost world, and nostalgia for a time when poets had the power to make one. Stevens gave this art its perfect epitaph, in "The Man with the Blue Guitar": "I cannot bring a world quite round, / Although I patch it as I can."

In the second half of the twentieth century, then, the poetry of world gave way to the poetry of earth. This poetry—our poetry —prefers to imagine the artist not as a creator, but as a witness. It has a strong sense of ethical obligation, believing that the poet must serve as a bearer of memories and perceptions that time would otherwise sweep away. Whenever a poet is concerned with giving things their proper names, or with remembering what everyone else forgets, or with seeing nature so intently that it seems to yield up secrets, he or she is practicing this sort of Heideggerian poetry.

What makes the poetry of earth so challenging to write is that poets are instinctive world-builders. The artistic imagination is imperial, seizing on things seen and turning them into occasions for symbol and metaphor. (Think of all the poems that have been written to wrest the bird's song away from the bird and turn it into a symbol of transcendence, freedom, or passion.) Clearly, resisting this tendency requires an austere ethical discipline. But for the poetry of earth to be more than a bare catalogue of things seen, for it to achieve the linguistic and emotional richness of great poetry, requires a specifically artistic discipline as well. The poet of earth must use language to make us notice what we usually ignore, the way Van Gogh draws our attention to a humble pair of shoes. But he must avoid constructing the kind of coercive, tendentious myth that Heidegger builds around those shoes.

In Seamus Heaney's sequence "Squarings," he is constantly brought up against the difficulty of such poised restraint. The first part of the poet's task, Heaney makes clear, is to remain attentive to what most people ignore. "Make your study the unregarded floor," he adjures, and the whole sequence is full of concrete, sensual images: "Scissor-and-slap abruptness of a latch. / Its coldness to the thumb. Its see-saw lift / And drop and innocent harshness." Heaney is unrivaled at this sort of "study," which carries out the Heideggerian task of bringing "beings to word and to appearance." And in "Squarings," he insists that capturing the sensual world is more than an aesthetic activity; it also has a spiritual significance. At certain moments, "seeing things"—the title of the 1991 book in which "Squarings" appears—means seeing through them and beyond them. Heaney's poem is a record of such epiphanies, moments when the sheer fullness of the earth seems about to overflow: "A phenomenal instant when the spirit flares / With pure exhilaration before death."

For Heaney, however, the poet can only be true to such exhilarating moments by respecting their strangeness. That is why the word "epiphany," which Joyce famously used, does not quite fit Heaney's conception. The word comes from the Greek for appearance or shining-forth; in the Christian calendar, the Feast of the Epiphany celebrates the appearance of Christ's divinity to the Magi. But for Heaney, it is by no means clear that it is God who is shining through the earth, filling it with His glory. All the poet can honestly say is that the earth itself appears to shine. Recording that radiance is the farthest he can go in the direction of prayer. That is why the language of Heaney's epiphanies is consistently negative, a matter of warding off conclusions and explanations. His sacred moments are those when "Nothing prevailed, whatever was in store / Witnessed itself already taking place / In a time marked by assent and by hiatus."

"Nothing prevailed" might be the Heideggerian poet's description of paradise: a moment of perfect restraint, when every being is allowed to be simply and wholly itself. This sense that "nothing" is more than an absence—that it can be a positive force, whose advent is to be welcomed—appears again in the work of Charles Simic, a poet clearly indebted to Heidegger. "Out of poverty / To begin again / / With the taste of silence / On my tongue," Simic writes in his poem "White," immediately plunging into the paradox at the heart of the poetry of earth. For if the poet's calling is to let beings be, then anything he says about them is a kind of violation of their integrity, and the best poetry would have "the taste of silence." Later in "White," Simic returns to this problem in a startling, homely, yet philosophically dense image:

In the inky forest,
In its maziest,

Murkiest scribble
Of words

And wordless cries,
I went for a glimpse

Of the blossomlike
White erasure

Over a huge,
Furiously crossed-out something.

The whiteness the poet seeks is an absence, but also the trace of a presence. It is the white not of void but of erasure, the silence not of muteness but of reticence. In these lines, Simic succeeds in capturing some of the genuine strangeness of the poetry of earth, with its self-canceling assertiveness. It is a contemporary version of the medieval *via negativa:* only what cannot be said is worth saying.

If Heaney and Simic demonstrate the exigent power of the Heideggerian mode, Billy Collins demonstrates that mode's comfortable decay. The poetry of earth succeeds only when it manages to make the earth itself strange to us, so that we can perceive it in its aloof beauty. When the poet allows the earth to remain familiar, however, his praise of it becomes mere praise for the familiar—for everything that is undemanding and reassuring. That is the note Collins strikes in "Earthling," where, after imagining what it would feel like to be heavier or lighter on other planets, he concludes: "How much better to step onto / the simple bathroom scale, / a happy earthling feeling / the familiar ropes of gravity." Collins turns the name of earth, which was an enigma to Heidegger, into a synonym for all that is "simple" and "happy." But he too is drawn, by the common impulse of our poetic moment, to the question of how poetry can do justice to the earth. In their different ways, many of our leading poets are trying to make us not just understand but experience the truth Heidegger stated in "The Origin of the Work of Art": "At bottom, the ordinary is not ordinary; it is extraordinary."

Poetry and the Problem of Politics

Poetry and politics seem like they ought to be opposites. Poetry, after all, is the realm of imagination; politics deals with the world as it is. Poetry is solitary, a transaction between reader and writer, while politics is practiced in the mass. As a result, poetry can be absolute, while politics is the art of compromise: there is no perfect law or perfect candidate, only better and worse ones. Finally, and most important, poetry is innocent—a bad poem never killed anyone—while politics is the realm of guilt, where a bad decision or an evil intention can result in the death of millions.

Why, then, should poetry and politics have anything to do with each other, any more than poetry and medicine, or painting and politics? Yet they always have, ever since Plato first began to worry about the relationship between them in Book III of the *Republic*, where Socrates discusses whether poets are to be allowed in the ideal city. The *Iliad*, with its tales of jealous and ambitious Olympians fighting each other through human proxies, was the poem that taught the Greeks how to imagine their gods. Yet Socrates argues that Homer cherishes all kinds of dangerous and absurd ideas about the gods: for instance, he portrays Zeus weeping over the death of Sarpedon, one of his favorite heroes. But weeping is exactly the kind of thing that a hero is not supposed to do. In the ideal city Socrates describes in the *Republic*, warriors will be raised to be hard and ruthless, so as to be effective in battle. "If our young people . . . listen to these stories," Plato writes, "without ridiculing them as not worth hearing, it's hardly likely that they'll consider the things described in them to be unworthy of mere human beings like themselves, or that they'll rebuke themselves for doing or saying similar things when misfortune strikes. Instead, they'll feel neither shame nor restraint, but groan and lament at even insignificant misfortunes."

Poetry, in Plato's view, is an inherently political matter because it has unavoidable public effects. If politics depends on cultivating the character of citizens, and poetry has a tendency to corrode that character, then poetry is a direct threat to the state. Indeed, Plato goes on to say that not just the subject matter of poetry but even its form and technique must be regulated by the government. He distinguishes between narrative, which tells a story in the poet's own words, and imitation, in which the poet speaks in the voice of one of his characters. Imitation, Plato argues, is an inherently debasing activity, because it leads the writer, and therefore the reader, to take on the form of contemptible characters and even inanimate objects, in a way that is ultimately degrading. "The more inferior he is," Plato observes, "the more willing he'll be to narrate anything and to consider nothing unworthy of himself. As a result, he'll undertake to imitate seriously and before a large audience all the things we just mentioned—thunder, the sounds of wind, hail, axles, pulleys, trumpets, flutes, pipes, and all the other instruments, even the cries of dogs, sheep, and birds."

For Plato, it's self-evident that this kind of promiscuous imitation—literature's ability to make us imagine our way into all kinds of lives and experiences—threatens the integrity of the self. That is why he advocates expelling poets, or at least the wrong kind of poet, from the ideal city: "If a man . . . should arrive in our city, wanting to give a performance of his poems, we should bow down before him as someone holy, wonderful, and pleasing, but we should tell him that there is no one like him in our city and that it isn't lawful for there to be. We should pour myrrh on his head, crown him with wreaths, and send him away to another city." Plato's rejection, clearly, is founded on a deep, even superstitious respect for the power of poetry, which he believes can deform our very sense of self.

Today, this is the kind of argument we are more likely to hear about, say, violent video games: a first-person shooter trains players to think of themselves as killers and desensitizes them to human life, which in turn leads to school shootings. The idea that poetry could have an equally serious effect on our souls now seems antiquated, simply because literature is no longer a cutting-edge entertainment technology. Movies and games seem more threatening because they are far more stimulating to the senses. But to Plato, a reading of an epic or a performance of a tragedy was exactly this kind of seductive and immersive experience; and he worried, as we still do, that what we imitate has the power to shape the kind of citizens we become.

This is one way that literature and politics confront one another. Literature offers an imaginative freedom that strikes the sober statesman as reckless and dangerous; a good society has to regulate literature because of its subversive power. Something of this tradition persisted until modern times in the form of censorship laws, which empowered the state to ban books it thought likely to lead citizens astray. But over the course of the twentieth century, free societies voluntarily gave up this power. One of the landmark texts in that process was the ruling of judge James Woolsey in the 1933 case "The United States versus One Book Called *Ulysses*." The very name of the case now sounds odd, barbaric: how could the government prosecute a book, much less a book like *Ulysses*?

But at the time, importing obscene books was illegal, and the publisher Random House deliberately provoked a prosecution in order to test whether *Ulysses* would be considered obscene or pornographic. Judge Woolsey's answer was no. Although the book contained degrading words and images—the very sort of thing that Plato demanded be banned—it should not be considered obscene, because everything Joyce wrote had a literary purpose. As Judge Woolsey wrote:

> Joyce has attempted—it seems to me, with astonishing success —to show how the screen of consciousness with its ever-shifting kaleidoscopic impressions carries, as it were on a plastic palimpsest, not only what is in the focus of each man's observation of the actual things about him, but also in a penumbral zone residua of past impressions, some recent and some drawn up by association from the domain of the subconscious. He shows how each of these impressions affects the life and behavior of the character which he is describing.

If a character in *Ulysses* thinks about sex or masturbation or defecation, it is not because Joyce wants to excite obscene thoughts, but because he is faithfully portraying the way our mental lives actually work.

This was a victory for literature, since writers and publishers no longer had to fear that "advanced" books would be confiscated by the post office. More, it was a victory for liberalism, because it endorsed the principle that free citizens can be trusted to understand complex and even dangerous ideas. Plato envisions the citizens of his *Republic* more or less like children, who are unable to make critical judgments about what they read. Citizens in a democracy, on the other hand, must be considered capable of reading a book like *Ulysses* without being deranged by it.

It's possible to wonder, however, if this modern tolerance for subversive books is merely a sign that we no longer share Plato's belief in the power of literature. For Plato, to read about something base was to invite baseness into our souls, like an infection. For Judge Woolsey, reading a text as literature means holding it at a certain mental distance, considering it hypothetically and objectively. In other words, literature becomes freer as it becomes less dangerous, and it becomes less dangerous as it becomes less powerful. We can afford to tolerate *Ulysses*, where Plato would not tolerate the *Odyssey*, because we no longer really believe that literature has the power to shape our souls.

In the twentieth century, it was only totalitarian societies like Nazi Germany that preserved the Platonic tradition of guarding the body politic against infection by literature. One of the early symbolic actions of the Nazis, after they took power in 1933, was to hold a series of public book-burnings, in which works by leftist, pacifist, and experimental writers were thrown into bonfires. At one such book-burning, the Nazi minister of propaganda, Joseph Goebbels, delivered a speech in which he announced, "The future German man will not just be a man of books, but a man of character. It is to this end that we want to educate you. As a young person, to already have the courage to face the pitiless glare, to overcome the fear of death, and to regain respect for death—this is the task of this young generation. And thus you do well in this midnight hour to commit to the flames the evil spirit of the past. This is a strong, great and symbolic deed." Here is the intimate connection between literature, education, and politics that Plato took for granted. If books shape citizens, then only the "right" books—which for the Nazis meant the most hateful books—can be allowed into the state. The tolerant indifference to literature we find in a liberal democracy is infinitely preferable to this kind of passionate involvement with literature.

Ironically, however, while the modern period saw the importance of literature shrink in the eyes of the state, it also witnessed an immense inflation of literature in the eyes of writers themselves. As literacy spread and mass culture emerged, serious imaginative literature reached an ever-decreasing share of the reading public. In the early nineteenth century, when the English Romantic poets were writing their masterpieces, their readership could be measured in the hundreds. Poets like Wordsworth and Shelley were regarded as impossibly difficult and eccentric, and were frequently mocked for their pretensions. Yet it was these very poets who began to believe that literature, far from being the pastime of an elite or a clique, was the most powerful expression of human destiny, including political destiny. For them, literature and politics were not adversaries, as Plato believed, but partners in imagination.

The greatest statement of this idea can be found in Shelley's 1821 essay "A Defense of Poetry." Shelley was born in 1792, in the third year of the French Revolution; his entire childhood and adolescence were spent in a world undertaking a great political experiment. For young people in the 1790s, it felt a little like the 1960s would feel to a later generation—a moment when the world was about to be reborn. Wordsworth gave this feeling its classic expression in the famous lines from his autobiographical poem *The Prelude*:

> Oh! pleasant exercise of hope and joy!
> For mighty were the auxiliars which then stood
> Upon our side, we who were strong in love!
> Bliss was it in that dawn to be alive,
> But to be young was very heaven!—Oh! times,
> In which the meagre, stale, forbidding ways
> Of custom, law, and statute, took at once
> The attraction of a country in romance!

Yet by 1815, when Shelley was twenty-three years old, this experiment had ended in a resounding failure. The radical freedom of the early years of the Revolution had given way to revolutionary terror, the dictatorship of Napoleon, and finally a restoration of the very Bourbon kings whom the Revolution had swept away. In England, too, these were years of conservative reaction, in which fear of revolution made the ruling class crack down on any sign of popular discontent. Shelley captured the mood in one of his most overtly political poems, "England in 1819," in which the idealism and excitement of Wordsworth's lines have given way to sullen anger and hatred.

Where can people look, in a time of political disappointment and repression, for sources of renewal? The surprising answer Shelley gives in "A Defense of Poetry" is that the source of hope is poetry itself. For poetry is not just a matter of iambic pentameter, and a poet is not just a person who has an unusual skill with language. A poet is defined by his power of imagination, of visionary insight; and this power can be applied to politics no less than to literature. Indeed, Shelley writes, the poet and the lawgiver are actually the same person under two different names:

> Poets, according to the circumstances of the age and nation in which they appeared, were called, in the earlier epochs of the world, legislators, or prophets: a poet essentially comprises and unites both these characters. For he not only beholds intensely the present as it is, and discovers those laws according to which present things ought to be ordered, but he beholds the future in the present, and his thoughts are the germs of the flower and the fruit of latest time.

The poet is for the modern world what the prophet and the philosopher were in ancient times: the person who sees into the essence of things, who knows what the world really is and how it should be. There is something like a spirit of history that determines what the future will bring, and the poet is the person who hears that spirit's voice and communicates it to the rest of humanity. Shelley was certain that the best poetry of his time—including, of course, his own—was imbued with the energy of the future. The Romantic poets offered a vision of human renewal that would eventually transform governments and societies. As he writes in the essay's conclusion: "Poets are the hierophants of an unapprehended inspiration; the mirrors of the gigantic shadows which futurity casts upon the present; the words which express what they understand not; the trumpets which sing to battle, and feel not what they inspire; the influence which is moved not, but moves. Poets are the unacknowledged legislators of the world."

Shelley risks sounding ludicrously grandiose. After all, there is something inherently comic about the idea of an unacknowledged legislator: if you issue edicts and nobody listens to them, you're not a lawmaker so much as a crank, like a doomsday prophet on a street corner. And certainly few people in 1821 were looking to Shelley, or to any other poet, for instructions on how society should be governed. Yet as the poet knew, history is shaped not just by governments and economic forces, but also—maybe above all—by ideas, which determine the limits of the possible and give people a sense of how the world is and should be. The ideas of liberation, progress, and equality, to which Shelley devoted his life and work, helped to fuel the French Revolution and would go on to drive human progress throughout the nineteenth century. One of his early poems, "Queen Mab," was intended to spread these ideals among the common people, by clothing them in the form of a fairy tale. Today, if you look for a text of this poem online, the first place you'll find it is on Marxists.org. This is only appropriate, since while Karl Marx thought of himself as a scientific economist, he can also be considered a poet in Shelley's sense—the creator of a myth of social order that went on to have immense real-world consequences.

In American poetry today, the reigning assumption is that the natural place of the poet is on the side of progress and liberation —that is, on the left. A good example of this consensus could be seen during the George W. Bush administration, which heedlessly invited a number of American poets to a White House poetry event in February 2003, on the eve of the invasion of Iraq. In response, the poets formed a group called Poets Against the War, which compiled thousands of poems protesting war in general and the Iraq War in particular. One thing that is notable about this episode is that Poets Against the War included all the poets; there was no group called Poets for the War. Many of the protestors voiced the belief that the nature of poetry and the nature of war are inherently opposed. Here are the concluding lines of a poem from that moment called "Complaint and Petition," by Hayden Carruth:

> Let us speak plainly. You wish to
> murder millions, as you yourself
> have said, to appease your fury. We
> oppose such an agenda—we, the people,
>
> artists, artisans, builders, makers,
> honest American men and women,
> especially the poets, for whom I dare
> to speak.

Who could quarrel with the sentiment Carruth expresses? The poem opposes love and honesty to mass murder, and it leaves no doubt on which side not just the American people but, especially, the poet must belong. Yet it is obvious that this is not a good poem. It reads like the prose you would find on an op-ed page, chopped up into lines; it has no metaphors, no interesting turns of phrase, no rhyme or meter. Shelley was certain that artistic power was connected to political righteousness, but the connection is clearly a complicated one, since righteous sentiments alone do not make an effective work of art.

To the essayist William Hazlitt, one of the great liberals of the early nineteenth century, this would have come as no surprise. Hazlitt was deeply committed to the values of the French Revolution, and as the Romantic poets grew older and more conservative, he continually attacked them for abandoning their political idealism. Yet Hazlitt acknowledged, to his own distress, that some of the greatest poems appear politically immoral. The beauty of their language is often lavished on characters and causes that are opposed to our rational convictions about goodness and progress.

Hazlitt made this observation in an essay on *Coriolanus*, which is now one of the least performed Shakespeare plays. Coriolanus is a brave and successful general during the time of the early Roman Republic, and his victories on the battlefield lead him to want to run for the office of consul, the chief magistrate of Rome. But this requires campaigning for the votes of the common people, and Coriolanus's enormous pride, as a soldier and aristocrat, prevents him from doing this. In fact, he can't hide his contempt for the common people, and in several speeches of crabbed, harsh, but passionate rhetoric, he denounces ordinary Romans as cowards, dogs, and mutinous rebels. When this results in his banishment from the city, Coriolanus defiantly joins the army of the Volscians, the enemies of Rome, and promises to destroy the city that rejected him. He is stopped at the last minute only by the intercession of his mother, Volumnia, which he can't resist, even though, by changing his mind and calling off the attack on Rome, he ensures his own death at the hands of the Volscians.

Hazlitt was disturbed by the way Shakespeare's plot and language conspire to make a heroic figure of Coriolanus, even though his political views are poisonously anti-democratic. Why, after all, should we want to take the side of a single arrogant aristocrat against the common people of Rome? Yet as readers and audience members, we do, and this led Hazlitt to theorize that poetry itself may be attracted to reactionary and anti-democratic politics. As he writes, "The cause of the people is indeed but little calculated as a subject for poetry: it admits of rhetoric, which goes into argument and explanation, but it presents no immediate or distinct images to the mind. . . . The language of poetry naturally falls in with the language of power."

Shelley believed that poetry was necessarily on the side of justice, but Hazlitt is not so sure. Justice, Hazlitt knows, is often a gray and tedious business. In a liberal democracy, it might look less like a courtroom drama, with a single culprit triumphantly exposed and punished by a righteous judge, than like a board of education meeting—a matter of complicated, boring problems with unsatisfying solutions. That is because liberalism puts the many above the one and right before might. It demands that we suppress our instinct to dominate and show off, our love of the grand and stupendous, and instead cultivate our reason and sense of fairness. In all these ways, liberalism is the exact opposite of poetry, which thrives on glorious depictions of extraordinary individuals.

It is because poetry is on the side of power, rather than justice, that epic poems so often glorify war—starting with the *Iliad* and continuing down to *Paradise Lost*, with its celestial fight between the angels and the demons. Indeed, *Paradise Lost* is a classic example of a poem in which the poet's attraction to sheer energy and particularity, to what Hazlitt called "the language of power," works against its explicit political and theological message. Milton's goal is, as he says in the poem's opening lines, to "assert eternal providence / and justify the ways of God to men": that is, he wants to teach his readers to trust in God's wisdom and justice. Yet the poem is built around a character—Satan, the fallen angel—who rebels against God's wisdom and justice. And the force of Milton's language is such that we cannot help being attracted to Satan, simply because he is a figure of enormous ambition and passion.

Satan, like Coriolanus, compels our admiration against our better judgment. Indeed, precisely because he is sinful, it is far easier for us, as sinners ourselves, to identify with him and understand his motivations than it is for us to understand the poem's

God, who remains inscrutable and remote. As William Blake famously observed, "the reason Milton wrote in fetters when he wrote of angels and God, and at liberty when of devils and hell, is because he was a true poet and of the devil's party without knowing it." Milton, an ardent Protestant, would have been horrified to think that his poem had actually justified Satan, rather than God. But Blake is making the same point that Hazlitt would make a few decades later. It is in the nature of poetry to be attracted to qualities like passion and striving, regardless of their motivation.

Blake, however, considered those very qualities not devilish but divine, and when he said Milton was of the devil's party, he meant it as a compliment. Shelley shared this judgment, writing that Milton's Satan was, as a moral being, superior to his God. Both of them were responding to the poem's depiction of Satan as a rebel against God's arbitrary power, as if Satan were one of the revolutionaries who tore down the Bastille and guillotined Louis XVI. To the Romantics, repression was the enemy and release was the solution—release of the very kinds of energies that poetry was supposed to embody. In this way, it was possible for the Romantics to dodge Hazlitt's challenge. Poetry may be on the side of energy, but since justice is also on the side of energy, this presents no moral or political problem. We need more Satans in the world, since Satan is satanic only when viewed through the lens of a traditional, oppressive, hypocritical morality. Seen rightly, he is a liberator.

When we turn to the poetry of modernism, however, this satisfying equation between energy and justice, and therefore between poetry and justice, falls apart in a disturbing way. Artistically, poets like T. S. Eliot and Ezra Pound were fighting on the side of progress. They wanted to cast off the sentimentality and formal regularity of Victorian poetry, in order to create poems as fractured, demotic, and haunted as the twentieth century demanded. In the process, they earned an extraordinary cultural authority: from the 1920s through the 1940s, T. S. Eliot was probably the most influential literary figure in the English-speaking world. Yet Eliot was also a political reactionary who dabbled in fascist thought and anti-Semitism, and whose political ideal was a homogeneous Christian society purged of free-thinkers and Jews. Pound was much worse: living in fascist Italy, he became an ardent supporter of Mussolini, and during World War II he broadcast anti-American propaganda on Axis radio.

It would be reassuring to be able to draw a neat line between Pound's poetry and his politics—to enjoy the energy of his art and dismiss the energy of his opinions. But Pound himself makes this impossible. The *Cantos* contain the same kinds of reactionary, fascist, and anti-Semitic ideas that filled Pound's essays and broadcasts. Nor do we even have the consolation of saying that the poems filled with evil ideas are the worst parts of the *Cantos*, as if we could strip away its excrescences and be left with its beauty. In fact, some of Pound's most sonorous and passionate lines express his most dubious ideas. In Canto 45, Pound rails against usury:

> with usura, sin against nature,
> is thy bread ever more of stale rags
> is thy bread dry as paper,
> with no mountain wheat, no strong flour
> with usura the line grows thick
> with usura is no clear demarcation
> and no man can find site for his dwelling.

This is not just beautiful, but effective: whatever usura may be, we can't help but be turned against it by Pound's invective. Yet usury, for Pound, was no literary conceit. It was his main charge against American and British democracy, which he saw as having destroyed the possibility of producing great artists, such as the painters he goes on to list in the poem: Piero della Francesca, Juan Bellin, Fra Angelico. Of course, the traditional target of the charge of usury were Jews, whom Pound saw at the center of the Anglo-American capitalist conspiracy. When he stood up for Mussolini and fascism, while slandering his own country, it was in the name of the very same artistic values he defends in this poem. And yet it is a great poem. This is the paradox that Hazlitt identified: greatness in poetry is not rationality or justice, but energy and specificity. A poem like the usura Canto is satanic, in the spirit of Milton's Satan—the detestable made glorious through the amoral power of language.

William Butler Yeats struggled with this amorality in his poem

"Ancestral Houses," written in 1923 during the Irish Civil War. The poem contemplates the mansions built in Ireland by Anglo-Protestant families, which were being burned down by Irish Republicans who saw them as symbols of oppression. Yeats, who had frequently glamorized the aristocratic past in his poems, is torn between the beauty of these houses and their political significance. Is it possible, he asks, that beauty itself is rooted in oppression, that the very splendor and scope we admire in such houses is simply a memorial of exploitation? As Yeats asks in the last stanza of the poem:

> What if the glory of escutcheoned doors,
> And buildings that a haughtier age designed,
> The pacing to and fro on polished floors
> Amid great chambers and long galleries, lined
> With famous portraits of our ancestors;
> What if those things the greatest of mankind
> Consider most to magnify, or to bless,
> But take our greatness with our bitterness?

Is there any way to resolve this paradox? Or must we conclude, with Walter Benjamin, that "every document of civilization is at the same time a document of barbarism"?

The high modernists believed in the prophetic power of art, just as Shelley did. The prophecies they issued, however, were not of progress and liberation, but of reaction and submission to authority. Later poets, while they acknowledged the greatness of the modernists, were determined not to go down the same political path. One of the first great statements of this determination in English poetry can be found in W. H. Auden's poem "September 1, 1939," whose title itself marks a new approach. Modernist masterpieces sought to transcend history; they took place in a realm of myth and symbol, not in the ordinary world that is measured by the calendar. It was because art was higher than history that it could try to shape history. Indeed, fascism can be understood as the attempt to mold society in the way that an artist creates a work. Auden's title, on the other hand, firmly locates the poet inside our common, historical world. To understand the poem, you have to know that September 1, 1939, was the date that the German army invaded Poland, starting World War II.

What is the poet's responsibility in such a historical crisis? Auden had already written, in an earlier poem, that "Poetry makes nothing happen"; the poet is not able to legislate for us or show us a political ideal. What he can do instead Auden explains in the poem's last stanza:

> Defenseless under the night
> Our world in stupor lies;
> Yet, dotted everywhere,
> Ironic points of light
> Flash out wherever the Just
> Exchange their messages;
> May I, composed like them
> Of Eros and of dust,
> Beleaguered by the same

Negation and despair,
Show an affirming flame.

We can picture "the just" like stars in the night sky, or like people holding candles in a dark field. In neither case can they banish the darkness; their light does nothing more than announce their own existence. History, the world of politics and power, unfolds without consulting them. But at least the poet is there, watching and writing down what happens, in order to console his contemporaries and to inform posterity. In a way this is a profoundly pessimistic image, suited to a moment of historical catastrophe, when it seems beyond the power of any single individual to make a difference. But one way of defining our time is as an age of catastrophe, when we all feel helpless in the face of overwhelming challenges to the very survival of humanity. At such a moment, we no longer trust poets who come to us as legislators. What we demand instead, the only poets we can believe in, are witnesses.

Night Thoughts

It's not by chance that the end of the Cold War coincided with the beginning of the global warming panic. When the prospect of annihilation by nuclear weapons receded, the anxiety that humanity had developed was conserved, by attaching itself to the prospect of annihilation by climate change. This was necessary because the fear of nuclear war had been tolerable only because of its very imminence. We fear death and pain when they are still remote, but the dying, or people who undergo massive trauma, are said to dissociate from their bodies as a defensive or anesthetic mechanism. Just so, humanity was able to live with the idea of its own annihilation only by experiencing this annihilation as nearly present, by living in its impending shadow, and thus inducing the hectic carelessness we feel in the face of inevitable catastrophe. When this shadow withdrew, the idea of annihilation became visible once again in its intolerable massiveness. It is possible to live in a world that is one minute from midnight, but not in a world that is an hour from midnight, because in that hour we feel that we have the power, and therefore the responsibility, to do something to avert the catastrophe. Global warming was the next-best apocalypse, allowing us to reinstate the imminence of the end.

Only the sense that nuclear war was imminent made us careful enough to avoid it. Anyone born before 1989 was raised with the dread of nuclear war, but those born after the Cold War never had to suffer this dread. That is why they are exactly the ones who will find it thinkable to engage in a nuclear war; and whatever is thinkable will eventually become actual. By this reckoning, the war should come when the post–Cold War generation is old enough to take charge of the world's governments and militaries—say, around 2039.

Americans bear last names from so many different languages, we forget the idea that a name was originally a description, a snapshot of a family at a moment in time. How far back would you have to go to find the original fat Gross, the teetotaling Bevilacqua? But if the adoption of a family name had been postponed to the next generation, the name would have been different. Like Adam and the animals in Eden: if he had waited another minute, the tiger would have been called something else entirely.

If myths are stories that serve as a culture's common reference points, then our problem is not that we lack myths, but that our myths don't last long enough, that they succeed each other too rapidly. For two thousand years, every European knew what the story of Helen, Agamemnon, and Paris meant. Today, everyone born between 1930 and 1960 finds a similar meaning in the story of Eddie Fisher, Debbie Reynolds, and Elizabeth Taylor, while those born after 1980 have never heard those names, but find just the same meaning in the story of Jennifer Aniston, Brad Pitt, and Angelina Jolie. On the other hand, the more rapidly a myth decays, the more solidarity it produces in the narrow cohort of those who recognize it. Duration is exchanged for depth. That is why Americans can experience an emotional bond based on the television shows that happened to be broadcast during their childhood. Each age group is as united in this way as the citizens of each Greek city used to be by their local gods.

It is hard to overcome the feeling that the lives of those in the distant past were not quite serious, that it was a mistake for those who lived them to suffer at all. Weren't they simply preparing and rehearsing for our present, which is the only time things can really be at stake? Enlightenment would be the ability to view our own lives in this way, as only accidentally present, on the way to becoming the history of some other now.

Life in the Greek polis must have been like spending your whole adult life in the company of people you met in high school or college, prolonging that early competition into the adult world of politics. Only the esteem or contempt of those you start competing with early on can be truly gratifying or mortifying, because only young people take competition seriously. Adults compete shamefacedly, since they are old enough to know that even real stakes—money, power, fame—are only pretend.

Alexander and Caesar stand for two types of ambition, romantic and classical. Romantic ambition bursts the world open, multiplying the available objects of longing. Its strength is that it wins the loyalty of others, who recognize that they can accomplish more through the hero than they would be able to on their own; without Alexander, no Ptolemy or Seleucus. Its weakness is that it is insatiable, and requires a hinterland of potential achievement that can never be exhausted this side of the grave: Alexander needs an Asia, and is destined to die there. Classical ambition, on the contrary, engrosses all the available rewards in a given system of honors: Caesar insists on holding the consulship year after year. Its strength is that it is achievable in this world, since the rules of the game make it possible for the victor to know when he is victorious. Defeating his rivals is more important to him than the conquest of new domains. Because this is a zero-sum game, however, the classical hero's rivals are forced to resent him and ultimately to destroy him if they are to flourish: Caesar must die on the Senate steps.

The pre-Socratics said that everything is water; today scientists say everything is thirteen-dimensional strings. Over 2,500 years, we have not come to know more, but we have learned the meaning of what we already knew—namely, that we do not know what is or why it is, and can only speak about it metaphorically. Progress consists of the refinement of the metaphor.

The plan for nuclear waste disposal at Yucca Mountain, in Nevada, includes an attempt to communicate to human beings in the distant future that it is dangerous ground. This must be done not verbally but through landscape engineering, with signs so basic that even in the absence of language they would be recognized—crevasses, stark mountains, threatening rock formations. The fascination of this idea comes from the way it encapsulates four truths. First, our injuries to the earth will long outlast our civilization: we can poison better than we can cure. Second, we know human civilization will end, that a time will come when nothing of our current world will be at all communicable to the future—a certainty no previous civilization has dared to express. Third, this negates the premise of culture, particularly literature, which assumes the continuity of mankind over time. And fourth, it is possible that the earth we inhabit is already marked in this way by signs that we can't read, which means that they have failed in their intent, as ours must. After all, haven't we forgotten where the angels with swords of fire stand guard?

Opponents of cloning and genetic engineering take their stand on the idea of human nature—that a life in which we are made, instead of being born, will in some way be inhuman. The problem is not that this is false, but that the future won't care, in exactly the same way that we don't care that our lives would be considered inhuman by our ancestors of five thousand or even five hundred years ago. Just look at the way we are always clean, feel so little pain, do so little real work, and never see the stars. Our progress is a betrayal of their ways, much as a child's growing up is a betrayal of his parents. To oppose cloning is actually to want to clone ourselves, morally and intellectually, into the future, to make the future resemble us exactly; while to endorse cloning is to recognize the inevitable, unbridgeable difference between ourselves and the future, as between ourselves and the past.

The common daydream of going back in time to kill Hitler rests on the premise that the twentieth century as it actually occurred was the worst-case scenario, so that any alternative would be better. But imagine a history in which Germany and Russia went to war just ten years later: they would both have had atomic weapons and surely would have used them, so the death toll would have been exponentially higher. It is possible to imagine that an angel trying to avert catastrophe from mankind would choose for the war and the Holocaust to take place, because all other possible outcomes would have been even worse. Such an angel would have to act knowing that he would never be thanked, only recriminated—because to thank him would be to acknowledge that the evil we committed was not the worst we could do, but the best.

Even the best human civilizations have done nothing more than reduce fear and want to anxiety and dissatisfaction. The utopian, revolutionary impulse declares itself as the desire to improve on this achievement, to go onward to happiness and plenitude. But its secret wish is to smash the partial victory of civilization, to return the world to its barbaric starting point. Only then will the partial victory that is all we can achieve once again become difficult and distant enough to seem worth striving for.

In bad times, people feel that whether they act or refrain from acting, they are guilty. In good times, people are equally guilty, but they feel they can ignore this fact with a good conscience.

The current fear over the loss of biodiversity is rooted in the sense that we are recklessly destroying what it took evolution so long to create. But life as it heretofore evolved was a survival of the fittest under conditions of nature. What will survive from now on is what is fittest for human use; our will has become the environment in which evolution takes place. In other words, human nature has superseded nature, and what we are really afraid of is the matriculation this represents—the responsibility of becoming nature. Yet this transformation was always coming, from the first time a human being made a fire or notched a stick. Nothing short of our destruction could have stopped us from becoming the new nature, since it is our nature to replace nature.

What accounts for our strange lack of interest in going back to the Moon—such a momentous achievement, which we simply abandoned and never even regret? The reason must be that new places are valuable only because they have not been smeared with the snail-trail of our presence. Now that we've been to the Moon it is desecrated, disqualified. And so our interest shifts to dark matter and dark energy, purely hypothetical substances which, by definition, we can never perceive or affect. Only where we are not is worthy of our interest and our hope.

Stefan Zweig at the End of the World

The careers of Stefan Zweig and Walter Benjamin offer a contrast so perfect as to become a parable. The two writers were contemporaries—Benjamin was born in 1892, Zweig in 1881—and both operated in the same German literary ecosystem, though Benjamin was from Berlin and Zweig from Vienna. Both reached their height of productivity and reputation during the Weimar Republic, and as Jews both were forbidden from publishing once Hitler took power. And both their lives ended in suicide: Benjamin took his life in 1940 while trying to flee from France to Spain, and Zweig died a year and a half later in Brazil, where he sought refuge after unhappy sojourns in England and America.

Yet the similarities end with their biographies. As writers, they could not have been more different, and their literary destinies were exact opposites. Zweig flourished during his lifetime, enjoying huge sales of his psychologically charged novels and popular historical biographies. Born with a fortune—his father was a textile manufacturer in Bohemia—he earned another fortune through his books, carrying into literature the bourgeois discipline and regularity that he inherited from his ancestors. *Three Lives*, the biography of Zweig by Oliver Matuschek, describes his annual production of books during the 1920s:

> Over time Zweig had evolved a taut and effective work schedule for the production of his books. The winter months were spent in assembling the material, the spring was used for working up the early drafts, so that the final draft could be completed during the summer and the manuscript then sent off to the publisher as soon as possible. This allowed the typesetting and proofreading to be completed in good time by the autumn, in order to get the printed and bound copies into the bookshops to catch the Christmas trade.

Benjamin, by contrast, was not remotely popular, nor would he have wanted to be. His audience was not the public at large but his fellow writers and intellectuals, who held him in the highest esteem; Bertolt Brecht, Hugo von Hofmannsthal, Theodor Adorno, and Gershom Scholem were among his friends and patrons. Zweig, whose books were best-sellers in several languages, was able to survive the loss of his German market and remain fairly prosperous. But for Benjamin the exile from Germany was devastating, and he spent the rest of his life in dire poverty. When the two men died, Zweig was one of the most famous writers in the world, Benjamin one of the most obscure.

Yet today there has been a reversal of their fortunes. It is Benjamin who has been canonized as one of the most important theorists of modernism, his works studied and debated and interpreted. He has become an emblem of the fate of the mind under fascism, not just a thinker but a kind of saint. Zweig, on the other hand, was until recently a cipher on the American scene, a name from history rather than a living presence. It is a literary tortoise-and-hare fable, whose familiar if unwelcome lesson is that the most serious, most difficult, most "highbrow" writing is usually what wins in the end.

In the twenty-first century, things have begun to change, with novels and novellas from Zweig's catalogue pouring back into print at a fast clip. But it is not clear that this surge of interest has been accompanied by any improvement in his critical standing. Zweig remains today, as he was during his lifetime, the tragic German Jewish émigré writer whom it is acceptable to disdain. In 2010, the critic and translator Michael Hofmann caused a minor sensation with an essay in the *London Review of Books* that attacked the long-dead writer with as much passion and invective as if he had been, say, Jonathan Franzen. "Stefan Zweig just tastes fake," Hofmann quipped. "He's the Pepsi of Austrian writing."

Hofmann was reviving an old tradition of intellectual sniping. *Three Lives* is packed with the nasty things that other writers had to say about Zweig, who was less gifted than they were but, infuriatingly, more successful. To Hofmannsthal, he was a "sixth-rate talent." Karl Kraus, told that Zweig had triumphed in all the languages of the world, replied, "except one"—a jibe at his German style. A satire published in 1920 described a creature called "the Steffzweig": "there are a few who still regard it as a living being. However the Steffzweig is an artificial creation, constructed for a writer's conference in Vienna from feathers, skin, hair etc. taken from all manner of European animals." Kurt Tucholsky summoned a whole world of pathetic mediocrity when he described a character this way: "Frau Steiner was from Frankfurt am Main, no longer in the first flush of youth, quite alone and dark-haired. She wore a different dress every evening, and sat quietly at her table reading refined books. In a word, she belonged to the readership of Stefan Zweig. Enough said? Enough said."

The saddest thing about all this abuse is that no one was quicker to acknowledge the scale of his gifts, or to defer to writers of superior talent, than Zweig himself. In 1933, when the Nazis started holding bonfires of books, Zweig was one of the authors consigned to the flames. It was, he said, "an honor [rather] than a disgrace to be permitted to share this fate of the complete destruction of literary existence in Germany with such eminent contemporaries as Thomas Mann, Heinrich Mann, Franz Werfel . . . and many others whose work I consider incomparably more important than my own." Hofmannsthal's references to

Zweig drip with contempt, and on several occasions he actively tried to sabotage Zweig's career. But in his memoir, *The World of Yesterday*, Zweig compares Hofmannsthal to Keats and Leopardi, and recalls with awe the first time he heard him speak: "I have never known conversation on such an intellectual level with anyone else."

One of the most important facts about Zweig is that he was perhaps even more passionate a collector than he was a writer; and what he collected were the manuscripts of Mozart and Beethoven and Goethe, the highest peaks of human genius. Zweig did not claim to dwell at that height himself, but he was gifted enough—and sufficiently imbued with the German-Jewish passion for *Bildung* or cultivation—to worship at the shrine of art. In *The World of Yesterday*, he writes rather more enthusiastically about his acquisitions—a manuscript page of *Faust*, the handwritten score of Schubert's "An die Musik"—than he does about his own books: "I was aware that in this collection I had created something that in itself was worthier to last than my own works."

Yet even Zweig's love of culture can become a charge in the indictment against him. For one thing, it can make him look like what Proust contemptuously called a *"célibataire d'art,"* one whose relations with art are passionate to the point of abjection, precisely because they are not truly creative. Certainly there is something alarming about the passage in his memoir where Zweig proposes, in all earnestness, that the great books are too long and need cutting:

I could not help wondering what exactly it was that made my books so unexpectedly popular. . . . I think it arose from a personal flaw in me—I am an impatient, temperamental reader. Anything long-winded, high-flown or gushing irritates me, so does everything that is vague and indistinct, in fact anything that unnecessarily holds the reader up . . . why not bring out a series of the great works of international literature, from Homer through Balzac and Dostoevsky to Mann's *The Magic Mountain*, with the unnecessary parts cut?

Balzac and Dostoevsky aside, it is certainly true that the strength of Zweig's fiction is its compression and intensity. He specialized in short novellas, the best of which have titles that get straight to the emotional point: *Burning Secret, Confusion.* (Many of these stories were made into successful movies, most famously Max Ophüls's *Letter from an Unknown Woman.*) Zweig, who was a friend of Sigmund Freud and wrote a biographical essay about him, is fascinated by primal scenes, moments when naive young people are initiated into the powerful and perverse forms that sexuality can take. In *Burning Secret*, a young boy accompanies his mother to a resort, where she begins a flirtation with a predatory nobleman. Like a detective, the boy is determined to figure out exactly what is going on with these strange grown-ups. What is the force that draws them together, and why do they seem not to want him around? The story's climax comes when the boy eavesdrops on his mother and the baron in the hallway at night and misinterprets their erotic struggle as an attempted murder—a primal scene gone terribly awry.

Similarly, in *Confusion*, a handsome young college student falls under the intellectual spell of his professor and decides that he will help the old man complete his long-unfinished magnum opus on the Elizabethan drama. But the student cannot understand why the professor blows hot and cold, alternately encouraging him and holding him at an ironic distance. Not until the student ends up in bed with the professor's young wife does his confusion begin to clear up: the professor, he realizes, is gay, and he is fighting his own attraction for the young man. The book concludes with the teacher's passionate confession to his protégé, in which Zweig combines an acute analysis of the psychology of teaching with a remarkably forward-thinking plea for sexual toleration.

Even Zweig's only full-length novel, *Beware of Pity*—written in the late 1930s, when he had fled Austria for England—is a novella at heart, focusing, once again, on the romantic education of a naive young man. Lieutenant Hofmiller is a cavalry officer in a small Hungarian town on the eve of World War I. At home in the barracks but ill at ease in society, Hofmiller commits a fairly innocent social blunder: at a party at the local nobleman's mansion, he invites the daughter of the house to dance, not realizing that her legs are paralyzed. Overcome with shame and pity, he enters into a strange and ultimately destructive relationship with the girl, Edith, allowing her to believe that he wants to marry her when in fact the idea terrifies him. Here it is emotional immaturity, rather than sexual immaturity, that must be outgrown during the painful transition to adult understanding.

Not for nothing, clearly, was Zweig a product of the Vienna of Freud, Arthur Schnitzler, and Egon Schiele. And if *The World of Yesterday* turns out to be Zweig's most lasting and important book, as it now seems, it is largely because of his rich evocation of Vienna's fin-de-siècle. The city that Zweig describes, the one in which he grew up and triumphed, was the Vienna of the educated Jewish haute bourgeoisie. It was only the wealth and the curiosity of this class, Zweig believes, that made the city's golden age possible: "the part played by the Jewish bourgeoisie in Viennese culture, through the aid and patronage it offered, was immeasurable. They were the real public, they filled seats at the theater and in concert halls, they bought books and pictures, visited exhibitions, championed and encouraged new trends everywhere with minds that were more flexible, less weighed down by tradition." His own movement from the mercantile middle class to the cultural elite, Zweig writes, was the ideal trajectory of all German Jewish families, mentioning Aby Warburg and Ernst Cassirer. He could have added Ludwig Wittgenstein or, indeed, Walter Benjamin.

This Jewish cultural assimilation was made possible, Zweig explains, by Vienna's love of the arts and its tradition of toleration: "Poor and rich, Czechs and Germans, Christians and Jews peacefully lived together in spite of the occasional needling remark." At such moments, however, the rose color of Zweig's nostalgia is impossible to ignore. For the Vienna he idealizes was the same city where anti-Semitism flourished, where Karl Lueger became mayor on an anti-Semitic platform, and where the young Hitler laid the groundwork for his plan to exterminate the Jews. If you take Zweig at face value, it is inexplicable how Vienna became, in the interwar period, the site of a virtual civil war between Social Democrats and fascists, or the city that wildly applauded the Anschluss in 1938. Zweig wrote *The World of Yesterday* in a feverish few weeks in the summer of 1941 in, of all places, Ossining, New York, where his peregrinations had briefly taken him. If Vienna was really, as Zweig writes, the home of "live and let live"—"a principle that still seems to me more humane than any categorical imperative"—why did he end up writing about it in Ossining?

Hannah Arendt zeroed in on these questions when she stingingly reviewed *The World of Yesterday* in 1943. Zweig, Arendt believed, was the victim of the same illusion that had plagued German Jewry since the Enlightenment, and eventually led to its destruction. This was the belief that culture could do the work of politics. Despite what Zweig thought, Arendt writes, he never really belonged to Austrian society, because no Jew was allowed to belong to it. Instead he belonged to an international society of the famous, and he believed that membership in this cultural elite would protect him. But Zweig's fate made clear that he had wagered his life on an illusion. "Without the protective honor of fame, naked and disrobed," Arendt concluded, "Stefan Zweig was confronted with the reality of the Jewish people."

Vienna at the turn of the century was the birthplace of many intellectual movements, none of which turned out to be more consequential than Zionism. Zweig started his career as a protégé of Theodor Herzl, but the Herzl who mattered to him was the literary editor of the *Neue Freie Presse*, not the Jewish nationalist. When Herzl published Zweig's first essay on the front page of Vienna's leading daily, when he was still a teenager, he felt that he had reached the summits of literature. In his memoir, however, Zweig is oddly evasive about the reasons why Herzl's Zionism made little impression on him. He observes only that he was turned off by the way Herzl, whom he saw as a king-like personality, was disrespected by his own followers: "the quarrelsome, opinionated spirit of constant opposition, the lack of honest, heartfelt acceptance in the Zionist circle, estranged me from a movement that I would willingly have approached with curiosity, if only for Herzl's sake."

The truth is that Zionism of any kind was never in the cards for Zweig, because of his deep conviction that being Jewish meant being in the vanguard of cosmopolitanism. "I see it as the mission of the Jews in the political sphere to uproot nationalism in every country, in order to bring about an attachment that is purely spiritual and intellectual," he wrote in 1919. "This is also why I reject Jewish nationalism. . . . Our spirit is cosmopolitan— that's how we have become what we are, and if we have to suffer for it, then so be it: it is our destiny." Zweig's hatred of all kinds of nationalism solidified during World War I, and he came to see literature as the only existing manifestation of the international brotherhood for which he yearned. When Zweig writes about his friendships with everyone from Romain Rolland to Rainer Maria Rilke to Émile Verhaeren, he is not boasting so much as demonstrating the living possibility of a modern republic of letters. What Arendt derided as a mere society of the famous was, in Zweig's view, a humanistic elite that preserved the highest values of liberalism.

The fact that Zweig lived to see this version of liberalism utterly defeated in Europe was, depending on how sympathetically you look at it, either his tragedy or his comeuppance. For how could any liberalism hope to survive divorced from democracy? A liberalism of the elite was doomed to be a social luxury; yet Zweig's experience as an Austrian Jew left him convinced that the masses had no love for toleration, free speech, and pacifism. On the contrary, the energy of the times seemed wholly opposed to these things, as Zweig recognized when he described the outbreak of popular enthusiasm in the first days of World War I: "The great wave broke over humanity so suddenly, with such violence, that as it foamed over the surface it brought up from the depths the dark, unconscious, primeval urges and instincts of the human animal—what Freud perceptively described as a rejection of civilization, a longing to break out of the bourgeois world of laws and their precepts for once and indulge the ancient bloodlust of humanity."

The profound pessimism of this view, and its implications for the liberalism that Zweig cherished, were not lost on him. Zweig's nonfiction is today much less read than his fiction, though many of these books were translated into English in the 1920s and 1930s, at the height of his fame. The most significant for understanding Zweig's political dilemma is *Erasmus of Rotterdam*, which he wrote in 1933, in the months after Hitler came to power. (It was the first of Zweig's books not to be published by his lifelong publisher, Insel Verlag, which had purged its list of Jewish authors.)

Zweig's *Erasmus* does not fulfill many of the duties of a biography; his historical works were always more about conjuring an atmosphere of intellectual drama than about telling a comprehensive story. As an essay on the fate of liberalism in an age of fanaticism, however, *Erasmus* is a powerful witness to its moment. The contrast between Erasmus, the moderate reformer and peacemaker, and Martin Luther, the belligerent and uncompromising man of faith, is transparently Zweig's way of contrasting his own cherished ideals with those of triumphant fascism. As he says in his memoir, the book "presented my own views in veiled form through the person of Erasmus."

Given this close identification, it is all the more remarkable that Zweig does not make a hero of Erasmus. Every word of praise for his subject's irenic, cosmopolitan humanism is balanced by a word of censure for his timidity and abstemiousness. Fifteenth-century humanists, like twentieth-century liberals, were out of touch with the people and unable to grapple with real-world problems: "though their realm was extensive," with outposts among the intelligentsia of every nation, "its roots did not go deep, it only influenced the most superficial layers, having but feeble relations with reality." Erasmus himself is sharply blamed for declining to attend the Diet of Worms, where he might have done something to bridge the gulf between Luther and the Catholic Church. "The absent are always wrong," Zweig concludes, and the rebuke is directed also at himself. He made Arendt's indictment before she did.

But the cowardice of Erasmus, if such it was, finally seems to Zweig like an inseparable component of a civilized character. It is for the barbaric Luthers to make war, while the civilized Erasmuses carve out niches of peace. No wonder he concludes that "the humanistic ideal, that ideal grounded upon breadth of vision and clarity of mind, is destined to remain a spiritual and aristocratic dream which few mortals are capable of dreaming." Sounding surprisingly like Benjamin, Zweig places his trust in defeated ideas as the only possible source of redemption: "An idea which does not take on material shape is not necessarily a conquered idea or a false idea; it may represent a need which, though its gratification be postponed, is and remains a need. Nay, more: an idea which, because it has failed to secure embodiment in action, is neither worn out nor compromised in any way, continues to work as a ferment in subsequent generations, urging them to the achievement of a higher morality."

It is only when seen in the light of his political ideas that Zweig's suicide becomes more than a personal tragedy. When Benjamin took an overdose of morphine in 1940, it was because, having been sent back across the border to conquered France, he believed that he was about to fall into the hands of the Gestapo. In 1942, however, Zweig had been out of the direct path of Nazism for eight years. Wisely or luckily, he had chosen not Paris but London as his refuge, which meant that he was not swept up in the fall of France like Arendt, Benjamin, and so many other Jewish refugees. Still, that disaster terrified him sufficiently to make him book passage to America in June 1940. Here, too, he could have found shelter, like Mann and Brecht and many other writers he knew. But by this point Zweig was so off-kilter, so traumatized by exile and terrified by war, that he made the irrational decision to move to Brazil, where he had earlier been given a hero's welcome when he visited on a tour.

Finally, even Brazil did not feel safe. Zweig was convinced that even if Hitler lost the war—and after Pearl Harbor, this began to seem possible—the world would never again be "the world of yesterday." What Zweig needed for his peace of mind was the ability to forget the world crisis, to withdraw like Erasmus into a private sphere of intellect and decency. But the twentieth century had made this impossible: "The greatest curse brought down on us by technology is that it prevents us from escaping the present even for a brief time. Previous generations could retreat into solitude and seclusion when disaster struck; it was our fate to be aware of everything catastrophic happening everywhere in the world at the hour and the second when it happened." Zweig came to believe that there was nowhere left to escape to, no place where the values he cherished could survive. His curse was that he died believing this; our good fortune is that he was wrong.

Non-Jewish Jews

Rosa Luxemburg and Isaac Deutscher

In the second half of the nineteenth century, the Polish town of Zamość produced two of the most extraordinary Jewish personalities of the age. The first was I. L. Peretz, the great Yiddish writer, best known to many readers for his bitter story "Bontshe the Silent." In that tale, Bontshe is a modern anti-Job, a humble Jew who suffers an endless series of injuries and humiliations, but never raises his voice against God. When he dies and goes to heaven, even the prosecuting angel can find nothing to say against him, and the judge promises to give him anything he might desire. But all Bontshe can think to ask for is a hot buttered roll—whereupon the angels "hang their heads in shame at this unending meekness they have created on Earth." Even in death, Peretz implies, Bontshe can't grasp the lesson that the judge imparts: "You never understood that you need not have been silent, that you could have cried out and that your outcries would have brought down the world itself and ended it."

If there was one reader who would have agreed wholeheartedly with this critique of passivity, who understood the right of the poor to cry out and remake the world, it was the other famous native of Zamość, Rosa Luxemburg. Starting as a teenager, Luxemburg devoted her whole life to overthrowing capitalism in Europe. As a theoretician, orator, and activist, she rose to a leading position in the socialist parties of Poland and Germany, and came to embody the hope—and, to her opponents, the dread—of Marxist revolution. To Lenin, whom she admired and criticized, she was "the eagle of the revolution"; to the German right, she was "Red Rosa," an anti-Semitic hate figure, good for frightening children. Her legend was sealed in January 1919, when she and Karl Liebknecht, her fellow leader of the communist Spartacus League, were assassinated by right-wing soldiers, with the connivance of Germany's nominally socialist government.

To Hannah Arendt, who was greatly influenced by Luxemburg, her murder was "the watershed between two eras in Germany; and it became the point of no return for the German left." With her death, it seemed in retrospect, the possibility of a humane and democratic communism in Germany was foreclosed. Indeed, from that day to this, whenever people want to rehabilitate communism from its legacy of dictatorship and mass murder, they are drawn to Luxemburg as a symbol of the path not taken. Leon Trotsky—who never got along with Luxemburg in her lifetime, perhaps because they were too similar—declared that his Fourth International, the organization he founded to combat Stalinism, would fight "under the sign of the three Ls"— Lenin, Luxemburg, and Liebknecht. After World War II, an influential group of anti-Soviet French Marxists named themselves "Socialism or Barbarism," after a slogan used by Luxemburg in a pamphlet attacking World War I. She was a natural favorite of the New Left in the 1960s. Today, Germany's Left Party, the organizational descendant of East Germany's Communist Party, has an educational wing named the Rosa Luxemburg Stiftung. For PR purposes, this is a much better name from the German communist past than, say, Walter Ulbricht.

Luxemburg's posthumous legend began to take shape in 1920, with the publication of *Briefe an Freunde* (Letters to a Friend). This small book consisted of twenty-two letters written to Sophie Liebknecht, Karl's wife, during the years 1916–1918, which Luxemburg spent in prison as an antiwar agitator. "Whoever knows only Rosa Luxemburg the fighter and the scholarly author," the publisher claimed at the time, "does not yet know all sides of her." The letters revealed the inner Rosa, "the richness of the inexhaustible wellsprings of her heart." Indeed, these letters go a long way toward explaining the reverence in which Luxemburg continues to be held by so many. Shut up in virtual isolation, physically ill, spiritually devastated by a world war that had destroyed Germany's socialist movement, Luxemburg finds courage and love in the little glimpses of nature she is allowed:

> What I see from my window is the men's prison, the usual gloomy building of red brick. But looking diagonally, I can see above the prison wall the green treetops of some kind of park. One of them is a tall black poplar, which I can hear rustling when the wind blows hard; and there is a row of ash trees, much lighter in color, and covered with yellow clusters of seedpods (later they will be dark brown). The windows look to the northwest, so that I often see splendid sunsets, and you know how the sight of rose-tinted clouds can carry me away from everything and make up for all else.

Coming from "Red Rosa," this kind of thing struck readers with the force of a revelation. Here was a revolutionary who loved flowers and birds, and Hugo Wolf's Lieder, and the poems of Goethe. This Luxemburg offers the strongest possible contrast with Lenin, who famously said, "I can't listen to music too often . . . it makes you want to say stupid nice things, and stroke the heads of people who could create such beauty while living in this vile hell. And now you must not stroke anyone's head: you might get your hand bitten off. You have to strike them on the head, without any mercy."

Gender surely plays a role in the idealization of Luxemburg. Though she never had children, she was often maternal about animals—above all, her cat Mimi, which she doted on. ("Poor Mimi . . . impressed Lenin tremendously," she writes after a visit in 1911. "She also flirted with him, rolled on her back and behaved enticingly toward him, but when he tried to approach her she whacked him with a paw and snarled like a tiger.") Indeed, her tenderness toward animals can sound like another face of her compassion for the poor and oppressed. The connection is almost explicit in a letter she wrote to Sophie Liebknecht in December 1917, describing the arrival at her prison of a military wagon pulled by water buffaloes:

> The soldier accompanying the wagon, a brutal fellow, began flailing at the animals so fiercely with the blunt end of the whip handle that the attendant on duty indignantly took him to task, asking him: Had he no pity for the animals? "No one has pity for us humans," he answered with an evil smile, and started in again, beating them harder than ever. . . . [The buffalo had] precisely the expression of a child that has been punished and doesn't know why or what for. . . . No one can flinch more painfully on behalf of a beloved brother than I flinched in my helplessness over this mute suffering.

In fact, however, Luxemburg would have been offended to be thought of as merely compassionate. That mute buffalo might be her version of Bontshe the Silent, but she herself was anything but meek. On the contrary, she was more like Peretz's judge, urging the workers of the world to turn it upside down. As it happens, Peretz makes one fleeting, and highly revealing, appearance in the biography of Luxemburg by Elizbieta Ettinger. A certain Polish socialist once paid a visit to her, and mentioned that he had taught himself Yiddish in order to communicate with the Jewish workers. Her response was furious: "Here is another madman, another *goy* who learned the Yiddish jargon." This led to a denunciation of "literature in jargon," and in particular "Peretz, that lunatic, who has the temerity to insult Heine with translation from the beautiful German language to that old-Swabian dialect, corrupted by a smattering of Hebrew words and garbled vernacular Polish."

This disdain for Yiddish as a "jargon" was typical of the educated Jewish bourgeoisie of Luxemburg's generation. She was born in 1871 as Rozalia Luksenburg, the youngest daughter of an assimilated Jewish family. Her mother, Lina Loewenstein, could allegedly trace her family line through seventeen generations of rabbis. But Lina's sacred texts were Goethe and Schiller, and the children were raised speaking Polish, not Yiddish. In Warsaw, where the family moved when she was two years old, Rosa attended a Russian-language gymnasium.

Already as a young girl, Luxemburg was involved in underground socialist politics. She once chided the ten-year-old daughter of a comrade, "At your age I didn't play with dolls, I made the revolution." This may have been an exaggeration, but only a slight one: she was eighteen when she had to flee Poland to escape arrest. (The story goes that she won over the border guard by saying that she was running away from her family, who were trying to prevent her from converting to Catholicism.) From 1889 until the end of her life, Luxemburg lived in exile—first in Switzerland, where she helped found a small Marxist party called the Social Democracy of the Kingdom of Poland and Lithuania (SDKPiL), then in Germany, where she became a leader of the much bigger and more influential Social Democratic Party (SPD).

In her ambitions and hesitations, the young Luxemburg could have been any man or woman from the provinces, newly arrived in the big city. In 1898, writing to Leo Jogiches, her lover and fellow SDKPiL leader, Luxemburg boasted of her triumphs in socialist Berlin:

> Incidentally, I'm making a very big impression here—at least on my landlady—and what is most astonishing, everyone sees me as being extraordinarily young, and they're amazed that I'm already so mature. . . . I feel as though I have arrived here as a complete stranger and all alone, to "conquer Berlin," and having laid eyes on it, I now feel anxious in the face of its cold power, completely indifferent to me.

The anxiety she kept to herself; it was her preternatural confidence that impressed the leaders of the SPD. Young, foreign, and female, still uneasy with the German language, Luxemburg made her name with blistering articles in the Party press and speeches at Party congresses. From the beginning, she fought for the two principles that defined her political creed. The first was her commitment to revolution, which put her at odds with the reformist tendencies in the rather staid SPD. In a series of articles, she savaged Eduard Bernstein, the "revisionist" socialist who argued that reforming capitalism was more important than overthrowing it. History, Luxemburg remained certain to the end, was on the side of the workers' revolution—even though the revolution, like the Messiah, kept on not coming. Her very last article, published in January 1919 after the failure of the Spartacus uprising in Berlin, declared: "The whole road of socialism—so far as revolutionary struggles are concerned—is paved with nothing but thunderous defeats. Yet, at the same time, history marches inexorably, step by step, toward final victory."

Luxemburg's second principle, a corollary of the first, was that class always trumped nationality as a political force. Nationalism, she insisted, was a purely bourgeois ideology, which the proletariat could never really share; the workers' only loyalty was to the international working class. This belief pitted the SKDPiL against the much more popular Polish Socialist Party (PPS), which combined socialism with a commitment to the independence of Poland. Luxemburg's doctoral thesis, *The Industrial Development of Poland*, used economics to argue that Polish independence was actually impossible, thanks to the interdependence of the Polish and Russian economies. "The struggle for the restoration of Poland [is] hopelessly utopian," she wrote in 1905. The only solution to Polish problems was "a socialist system that, by abolishing class oppression, would do away with all forms of oppression, including national, once and for all."

It did not escape anyone's notice that Luxemburg, like Jogiches and most of the other leading figures in the SDKPiL, was Jewish, or that this might have something to do with their failure to share in the national aspirations of most Poles. An especially vicious campaign was launched against Luxemburg in 1910, when a Polish newspaper used obscene anti-Semitic rhetoric to discredit the SDKPiL. Luxemburg's party, the paper said, was "tied by race and family to the rest of the Jews; these purely anthropological ties are so strong that anyone who dares to question the ideology of any Jew is immediately confronted by an alliance of a Talmud Jew, a socialist Jew, and a liberal Jew."

In response, Luxemburg solicited letters of support from leading Western European socialists. Writing to a Belgian party leader, she explains, "the entire liberal, progressive press has abandoned itself to an all-out orgy of anti-Semitism. . . . As you see, it is a Dreyfus case in miniature." Yet in the articles Luxemburg herself wrote about the Dreyfus Affair, it is striking how consistently she refused to view the case in Jewish terms—for instance, when she describes "militarism, chauvinism-nationalism, anti-Semitism, and clericalism" as "direct enemies of the socialist proletariat." Even explicit anti-Semitism, it appears, cannot really be directed against the Jews, only against the proletariat. Class, not nation or religion, is the only genuine reality.

Clearly, the anti-Semitic slander against Luxemburg was the exact reverse of the truth. Not only did she not represent a secret alliance between religious, liberal, and radical Jews; she was actually much more hostile to Jewishness, in any form, than she was to other expressions of nationhood, especially Polish ones.

Writing to Jogiches about a visit to Upper Silesia in 1898, she rhapsodizes about Poland in terms that are anything but scientifically Marxist:

> The surroundings here have made the strongest and most emphatic impression: cornfields, meadows, woods, broad expanses, and Polish speech and Polish peasants all around. You have no idea how happy it all makes me. I feel as though I've been born anew, as though I have the ground under my feet again. I can't get enough of listening to them speak, and I can't breathe in enough of the air here!

Compare her reaction to "Polish speech" with her reaction to "Yiddish jargon," and you can gauge Luxemburg's profound discomfort with everything Jewish. When she visited a resort in 1904, for instance, her pleasure at encountering "a genuine [party] comrade, a living and breathing one from Berlin," turned to pain when she discovered that "unfortunately, he was also an even closer comrade in the sense of the faith of our fathers."

This disdain had political consequences as well as personal ones. Early on, when Luxemburg's SDKPiL was a minor party whose leaders were mostly in exile, the Jewish Bund was one of the biggest socialist parties in Eastern Europe. Other Russian and Polish party leaders wanted to make an accommodation with the Bundists; Luxemburg disagreed, in accordance with her internationalist views. But there is more than principle at work in her unusually abusive descriptions of Bund leaders as "rabble" and "the shabbiest of political horsetraders." In German, the word she used was *Schacher*, "haggler," a term that carried strong anti-Semitic connotations, and was used as such by Marx in his notorious essay "On the Jewish Question."

Luxemburg's fullest statement on the Bund comes in a letter to a Polish comrade in 1901:

> Well, now, to put it briefly, this entire "Bund" . . . what they deserve at the least is to have any upstanding, respectable person throw them down the stairs the minute they open the door (and for this purpose it is best to live on the fourth floor) . . . they are individuals who are made up of two elements: stupidity and cunning. They are incapable of speaking two words to anyone without having the concealed intention of robbing them (in a moral sense).

Luxemburg's political career was defined, in large part, by her struggle against the PPS, but she never writes about the Polish socialists in such venomously personal terms. It is unmistakable that Jewishness—even in the anti-Zionist form of the Bund's Jewish socialism—provoked in Luxemburg a visceral need to disassociate herself. Seen in this light, there is something more than simple humanitarianism at work in the famous lines she wrote from prison in 1917:

> What do you want with this theme of the "special suffering of the Jews"? I am just as much concerned with the poor victims on the rubber plantations of Putumayo, the Blacks in Africa with whose corpses the Europeans play catch. . . . Oh that "sublime stillness of eternity," in which so many cries of anguish have faded away unheard, they resound within me

so strongly that I have no special place in my heart for the [Jewish] ghetto. I feel at home in the entire world, wherever there are clouds and birds and human tears.

Ironically, these lines were addressed to Mathilde Wurm, who was Jewish, as were almost all of Luxemburg's closest friends and party comrades. According to Arendt, writing about Luxemburg's "peer group" in *Men in Dark Times*, "these Jews . . . stood outside all social ranks, Jewish or non-Jewish, hence had no conventional prejudices whatsoever, and had developed, in this truly splendid isolation, their own code of honor." Even today, there are many Jews who admire this definition of Jewishness as a universal humanism, which prides itself on indifference to specifically Jewish interests. But Luxemburg's own words offer less support to Arendt's view of her than to the view of Jacob Talmon, who wrote that Luxemburg's "all-pervasive revolutionary internationalism appears to me an expression of the Jewish malaise of an outsider."

More, it represents a failure of empiricism—an inability to reckon with the factors that shape political and psychological reality, for Jews and non-Jews alike. This failure exacted a large toll on Luxemburg's political work, and falsified her hopeful prophecies. She viewed the Eastern European proletariat in wholly idealized Marxist terms: "The highest idealism in the interest of the collectivity, the strictest self-discipline, the truest public spirit of the masses are the moral foundations of socialist society, just as stupidity, egotism, and corruption are the moral foundations of capitalist society."

But this was the common people as it should be, not as it was. One might say that Luxemburg failed to connect her proletarian ideal with the real soldier she saw whipping a helpless buffalo —a man brutalized by the war that was supposed to have radicalized him. The same mistake is what allowed her to tell Sophie Liebknecht, in late 1917, that the Russian Revolution could not possibly be dangerous for the Jews: "As far as pogroms against Jews are concerned, all rumors of that kind are directly *fabricated*. In Russia the time of pogroms has passed once and for all. The strength of the workers and of socialism there is much too strong for that. The revolution has cleared the air so much of miasmas and stuffy atmosphere of reaction that a new Kishinev has become forever passé. I can sooner imagine pogroms against Jews here in Germany." She was half right.

Isaac Deutscher lived from 1907 to 1967, a period of Jewish history as eventful as any in the previous two thousand years. Born near Cracow to a family of Gerer Hasidim, he became one of the world's foremost Marxist journalists and historians. This was a journey, as he himself understood it, from the middle ages to modernity, from dusty superstition to cutting-edge historical science. *The Non-Jewish Jew*, a collection of Deutscher's essays on

Jewish subjects that first appeared in 1968, begins with a biographical sketch by his widow, Tamara Deutscher, organized around the image of vaulting a historical gulf. "That gulf was so immense that it baffled and fascinated him," she writes. "It both amazed and amused him" that his early memories belonged to the same person as his adult achievements. How did the boy "with a thick black crop of hair [and] curled sidelocks," knocking timidly on the rabbi's door to wake him for morning prayers, become the radical orator who addressed a crowd of fifteen thousand students at a Berkeley teach-in?

Practically the only source for Deutscher's early life is this memoir, "The Education of a Jewish Child," which quotes him extensively and seems to be his own authorized version. While it documents a journey away from Judaism, it is a text strikingly crowded with Jewish echoes. For instance, it tells the story of Isaac's great-grandfather, whose "fanatic convictions" led him to prohibit his son from becoming a Hasid. The son, Isaac's grandfather, was desperate to join the court of the Gerer Rebbe, but when he set out on the journey, his father moved heaven and earth to stop him, even calling in the Austrian police. This is very much like the story that Nachman of Bratslav told under the title "The Rabbi's Son," in which a father repeatedly thwarts his son's efforts to join a Hasidic rebbe. At the end of the tale, we learn that the omens which appeared to support the father's ban were actually the work of Satan, and that the meeting, which never took place, would have brought about the coming of the Messiah.

The rebellion of Deutscher's grandfather was archetypal, and so was his own. Indeed, his story reads like a classic *maskil*'s autobiography; he could be Solomon Maimon talking about Lithuania in the 1760s. Deutscher, too, was a Talmudic prodigy who grew disillusioned with his learning, and finally contemptuous of it. At the age of thirteen, Tamara Deutscher writes, Isaac delivered a discourse about the *kikayon*, "a bird [that] is big and beautiful and unlike all other birds," which appears once in seventy years and whose saliva has miraculous curative powers. The question the young Deutscher had to answer, drawing on a multitude of authorities, was whether this saliva was kosher—and he did this so impressively that he was immediately ordained a rabbi.

So what if the *kikayon*, in the Bible, is not a bird but a plant, the "gourd" that God causes to grow to shelter Jonah? So what if, as Bernard Wasserstein has pointed out, this account bears no relation to how rabbis were actually ordained? Whether the mistakes and exaggerations were Tamara's or Isaac's, the story served to communicate the desired message: nothing could be more foolish, more of a waste of intellectual power, than traditional Judaism. At the age of fourteen, Tamara's memoir continues, Isaac confirmed his break with religion with a spectacular blasphemy. He taunted God by eating a ham sandwich, over a rabbi's grave, on Yom Kippur. When no bolt from the blue followed this triple sin, he knew that God did not exist. (Still, he was afflicted with terrible guilt, less on God's account than on his parents': "At the family table I could hardly lift my eyes. I had never felt more remorseful in all my life.")

As a teenager, Deutscher plunged into Polish literature, writing poetry and criticism and translating Thomas Mann. In 1927, at the age of twenty, he joined the Polish Communist Party and served as the editor of its clandestine press. But he turned out to be a premature anti-fascist. In 1932, he published an article warning of the threat of Nazism, at a time when the Communists still regarded the Social Democrats as the main threat. Deutscher was expelled from the Party, which turned out to be a blessing in disguise, since most of the Polish Communist leadership was murdered by Stalin in 1938.

This series of events turned Deutscher into a strong critic of Stalinism, but didn't shake his allegiance to Marxism or to the ideal, as opposed to the real, Soviet Union. He managed to escape Poland at the last moment, moving to London in April 1939 as a correspondent for a Zionist newspaper. After a brief, unhappy attempt to serve in the exiled Polish army, Deutscher remade himself, in an amazingly short period of time, into an English journalist, joining the staff of the *Economist*. After World War II, he became a leading pundit on Soviet and Eastern European affairs, a position bolstered by his groundbreaking biographies of Stalin and Trotsky. For two decades at the height of the Cold War, Deutscher flourished as a sympathetic but critical interpreter of communism to the West.

In Deutscher's own view, his journey from Hasidism to communism was a demonstration of the power of enlightenment. Yet his utopian hopes were continually falsified by reality, especially when it came to the situation of the Jews. Instead of emancipation, the modern world had brought the Jews of Europe to the brink of annihilation. Instead of ending anti-Semitism, the communist regime in Russia mounted veiled attacks on Zionists and rootless cosmopolitans. And in an era when Marxist theory predicted the decline of the nation-state, the fate of the Jews came to depend on the flourishing of Israel, a Jewish state. Faced with such contradictions, Deutscher was forced to deploy all his dialectical ability, and a certain amount of sheer evasion, to keep faith with the Marxism he cherished.

In his essay "The Russian Revolution and the Jewish Problem," for instance, Deutscher writes ruefully that "the Bolsheviks took an over-optimistic view of the chances of solving the Jewish problem." There are two premises taken for granted in this formulation: that the existence of Judaism was a problem, for which a solution was needed; and that Russian communism was sincerely dedicated to eradicating anti-Semitism. If it failed, Deutscher believes, this was due partly to the deep roots of Christian Jew-hatred, and partly to the Jews themselves. For, Deutscher suggests, how could gentiles help noticing that Jews shirked combat duty in the Red Army, that they engrossed white-collar and

managerial jobs in the new Soviet state, and that they were stub-
bornly addicted to "the art and the tricks of petty commerce"?
As for Stalin's postwar paranoia about the Jews, was it not justified by the fact that "the Jews in Russia had a penchant, so to
speak, for America and for their relatives there"? If American
armies had marched into Moscow, wouldn't the Jews have been
"collaborators"? In this way, Deutscher manages to validate both
the communist and the anti-communist attacks on Jews in Eastern Europe. They attracted hatred because they were too prominent in the Party, and they attracted hatred because they didn't
love the Party enough.

In any case, Deutscher believed, the only solution to the fail-
ings of communism was more communism, but the right kind
this time—internationalist and revolutionary, rather than Stalin-
ist and Russian-nationalist. This is the communism to which
Deutscher converted as a young man, and "converted" is the
right word. For while Deutscher believed that his life had been
a journey from Jewish superstition to Marxist reason, it is easy to
see that it was really the exchange of one faith for another. These
faiths were convertible, for Deutscher as for many others, because they actually had much in common. Both were messianic,
looking forward to a time when all the evils of life—human life,
but specifically Jewish life—would be abolished. Both combined
intellectual subtlety with emotional exhilaration. Both were based
on a canon of sacred texts—the Torah, Marx's Paris Manuscripts
—that demanded close exegesis and study. Both looked to char-

ismatic leaders as embodiments of a sacred process—the Gerer Rebbe, Lenin.

Strictly speaking, in communism there is neither Jew nor Greek. Yet Deutscher did not stop thinking of himself as a Jew even when he became a historical materialist. Considering the world he lived in, and the events he lived through, this is hardly surprising. But it raised a significant personal and ideological problem for him: what makes a person a Jew if he no longer believes in Judaism? "To me the Jewish community is still only negative," he writes in the essay "Who Is a Jew?" "Religion? I am an atheist. Jewish nationalism? I am an internationalist. In neither sense am I, therefore, a Jew." Yet in some other sense, he was one. How could this be?

Practically speaking, Deutscher concludes, what keeps him a Jew is anti-Semitism. This was not a new idea—Spinoza said much the same thing, as did Theodor Herzl—but in the wake of the Holocaust it took on a new urgency. Now it was not just the fact of anti-Semitism that precluded assimilation; what was more, the memory of the victims of Nazism made the hope of assimilation look deeply dishonorable. Deutscher would have laughed at the religious terminology of Emil Fackenheim's 614th commandment—do not give Hitler posthumous victories—but he shared it intuitively. "I am, however, a Jew by force of my unconditional solidarity with the persecuted and exterminated," he concludes in "Who Is a Jew?" "I am a Jew because I feel the Jewish tragedy as my own tragedy." In the same essay, Deutscher also writes that "Nazism was nothing but the self-defense of the old order against communism," but it is as a Jew, not as a communist, that he experiences the pain and disgrace of the Nazis' crimes.

If one rejects both of the traditional definitions of Jewishness, as a religion and a nation, and yet still feels oneself to be inescapably Jewish, how can that feeling be given content and coherence? It is the continuing salience of this question that makes Deutscher a relevant figure long after his death, and the death of Soviet communism. His essay "The Non-Jewish Jew" has become famous because, in the Hegelian spirit Deutscher knew so well, it performs a brilliant dialectical reversal. Being hostile to Judaism, he concludes, does not make one a bad Jew; on the contrary, it makes one the best Jew of all. That is because the essence of Judaism lies not in obedience to God or Law, or in identification with a people, but in heresy. True Judaism is the faith that rejects Judaism.

Deutscher begins his argument by reaching back to his Talmudic training and recalling the figure of Elisha ben Abuyah, the heretical sage known as Acher, "the other." Acher appears several times in the Talmud as a Jewish authority who was also a student of Greek ways, and who broke with the rabbis in some profound but unspecified manner. In a famous story—which Deutscher does not cite, though he surely knew it—Acher is one of the four sages who enters the Pardes, the orchard of paradise, where he was unable to bear what he saw and "uprooted the plants." For Deutscher, however, he looks more like a noble adventurer, someone who "rode beyond the boundaries." "What made him transcend Judaism?" Deutscher asks.

The question is loaded, of course; the Talmud does not speak of Acher as someone who transcended Judaism, but as someone who vandalized it. But Deutscher is sure that Acher represents the best Jewish tradition, the one that also includes "Spinoza, Heine, Marx, Rosa Luxemburg, Trotsky, and Freud. . . . They all found Jewry too narrow, too archaic, and too constricting. They all looked for ideals and fulfillment beyond it." The freethinkers and revolutionaries he cites experienced Judaism as a prison or a ghetto, because they wanted to belong to another, more capacious community: the community of humankind.

What they did not recognize, and Deutscher doesn't recognize, is that Jews already belong to that community, even if they are not heretics. There is no such thing as a human being who is immediately universal. Home, as T. S. Eliot wrote, is where we start from, and Judaism is as good a place to start as any other. What really unites the great figures in Deutscher's canon is that they believed that there was something particularly disqualifying about Judaism as a habitation of the universal. Deutscher praises Freud, for instance, because "the man whom he analyzes is not a German, or an Englishman, a Russian, or a Jew—he is the universal man . . . whose desires and cravings, scruples and inhibitions, anxieties and predicaments are essentially the same no matter to what race, religion, or nation he belongs." But of course, the people whom Freud analyzed were mainly Jews. This does not necessarily mean they did not have the same "desires and cravings" as everyone else—though then again, maybe it does mean that. How would we know, unless we took the fact of their Jewishness seriously, rather than immediately and anxiously "transcending" it?

For Deutscher, the rejection of Jewish particularity in the name of what he calls "universal human emancipation" is Judaism at its best. "I hope," he writes in the essay's peroration, "that, together with other nations, the Jews . . . will find their way back to the moral and political heritage that the genius of the Jews who have gone beyond Jewry has left us." Logically, however, this makes no sense. The Jews who went beyond Jewry could not have accomplished this feat if there was not a Jewry to go beyond. A society made up entirely of heretics is as unimaginable as a society made up entirely of revolutionaries; the prestige of the exception requires that it be exceptional. And there is something unseemly about claiming that prestige for oneself. Saying that one is a Jew in the tradition of Spinoza and Heine is rather like saying that one is a Christian in the tradition of Kant and Beethoven: nice work if you can get it, but almost no one can.

But the real problem with the ideal of the "non-Jewish Jew" is that it is not, as it claims to be, an idea that transcends religion in the name of humanity. It is, rather, a restatement in secular terms of one of the most profound dynamics in European culture. This is the movement from letter to spirit, from law to love, from particular to universal, that is at the heart of the self-understanding of Christianity. Deutscher carefully avoids this comparison by choosing Acher, rather than Jesus, as his preferred Jewish heretic. But whenever a Jew tells other Jews that they are merely concerned about themselves, while he cares about the redemption of all mankind, he is recapitulating the original anti-Jewish movement of Christian theology. That is why any theologian could say of Christianity exactly what Deutscher says about Spinoza, that his thought was "Jewish monotheism carried to its logical conclusion and the Jewish universal God thought out to the end; and once thought out to the end, that God ceased to be Jewish." Contemporary philosophers like Alain Badiou and Slavoj Zizek have not failed to pick up on the symmetry of Christian anti-Judaism and Deutscher's Jewish anti-Judaism. They have embraced the idea of the non-Jewish Jew because it gives anti-Judaism an impeccably Jewish pedigree, and thus immunizes it against the charge of anti-Semitism.

But reading Deutscher shows that this is a thin distinction. In "Who Is a Jew?" he writes, "it is strange and bitter to think that the extermination of six million Jews should have given a new lease of life to Jewry. I would have preferred the six million men, women, and children to survive and Jewry to perish." Jewry—that is, Jewishness—deserves to perish, Deutscher believes, because Marx was right, and Judaism is just another name for capitalism. Thus his Marxist millennium would mirror the Nazi millennium: both would be *Judenrein*. The inability of Western thought to imagine an ideal society that is not predicated on the elimination of Judaism is the great and perpetual danger for Jews who live in that society. We don't escape that danger by clamoring to eliminate ourselves.

Angels of Liberalism

It is no wonder that Jews tend to be intensely patriotic Americans, or that our reading of American history is generally optimistic. We tell ourselves that there was anti-Semitism in America, but it went away; that America hesitated to fight Hitler, but eventually defeated him. When Jewish liberals are critical of America, it is usually in a spirit of disappointed love: we want the success of our American experience to be extended to everyone. The great American Jewish liberal question is Allen Ginsberg's "America when will you be angelic?" We want America to be angelic because we know it can be.

That is why one of the most authentic works of the American Jewish spirit is Tony Kushner's play *Angels in America*, whose twenty-fifth anniversary was celebrated in 2018 with a Broadway revival and the publication of an oral history, *The World Only Spins Forward*. Literature is news that stays news, and much of what Kushner saw about America in the 1980s—the action of the play takes place in 1985–86—is still part of our reality. Donald Trump himself is a 1980s figure; he's not mentioned in *Angels*, but the play's villain, Roy Cohn, was Trump's mentor and in some ways his role model. "This is intestinal is what this is, bowel movements and blood-red meat! This stinks, this is *politics*, Joe, the game of being alive," Kushner's Cohn rants, and what could be more Trumpian than the sense of politics as an amoral power game? In the relationship between Cohn and Joe Pitt—an idealistic Mormon conservative who thinks that voting Republican means standing for freedom and justice—Kushner offers a weirdly apt prophecy of the way Donald Trump seduced the conservative movement.

At the same time that he is attacking conservatism from without, however, Kushner is also powerfully questioning liberalism from within. *Angels in America* has been produced around the world, yet it remains highly specific, even local, in its Jewishness, its New York–ness, and its politics. Kushner takes it for granted that his audience will share his political landmarks, his pet martyrs (Julius and Ethel Rosenberg) and villains (Joe McCarthy, Ronald Reagan). Not until fairly late in the play does the audience hear any explicit explanation for what Roy Cohn did during the 1950s that made him so politically loathsome. Kushner counts on us to know why Cohn is someone we should love to hate, much as Shakespeare counted on his audience to know why Richard III was a bad guy.

One reason why *Angels in America* feels like a classic, however, is that the play is more complex and mysterious than its own politics. Louis Ironson, the main Jewish character, is clearly Kushner's surrogate in the story. It is Louis who offers the Broadway audience the expected attacks on Republicans; but he also allows Kushner to call some basic progressive assumptions into question. For Louis believes so strongly in progress, in the arc of history bending toward justice, that he cannot function when AIDS plunges him into a different reality. His abandonment of his sick partner, Prior Walter, is cast explicitly as a sin of ideological shallowness, in a scene where he offers a confession to an elderly rabbi:

> Maybe because this person's sense of the world, that it will change for the better with struggle, maybe a person who has this neo-Hegelian positivist sense of constant historical progress towards happiness or perfection or something, who feels very powerful because he feels connected to these forces, moving uphill all the time. . . . Maybe that person can't, um, incorporate sickness into his sense of how things are supposed to go.

A catastrophe like the AIDS epidemic cannot be fit into a progressive picture of American society or of human life. It is one of those moments when, as Theodor Adorno said in *Minima Moralia*, "the whole is the false"—his own pessimistic revision of Hegel, for whom the whole was the true. The idea that everything that is, is valid, because it is leading to a necessary consummation—despite all the losses and wrong turnings along the way—lies at the heart of liberal progressivism. For Kushner, AIDS refutes it, just as the Holocaust refuted it for Adorno.

While Kushner is careful not to compare these two disasters, his central image of the Angel inevitably draws a connection, by invoking Walter Benjamin's Angel of History. For Benjamin, the Angel of History was necessary precisely because there was no goal or direction to human affairs: "Where *we* see the appearance of a chain of events, *he* sees one single catastrophe, which unceasingly piles rubble on top of rubble and hurls it before his feet." Yet as a divine being, the angel also holds open the possibility that God will intervene to avert the stern decree of history. "The future did not, however, turn into a homogenous and empty time for the Jews. For in it every second was the narrow gate, through which the Messiah could enter," Benjamin writes at the conclusion of his "Theses on the Philosophy of History."

The power of *Millennium Approaches*, the first half of *Angels in America*, lies exactly here, in the way Kushner creates a sense of imminent and inexplicable redemption. Prior Walter, who is dying of AIDS and no longer has any grounds for hope, is the one figure in the play to whom the Angel can and must appear. The fact that he is not Jewish, but the scion of a very old WASP family, is one of Kushner's ways of insisting on the universality of the Jewish concept of the Messiah. The play believes that we are all living in a Jewish universe. (One of Prior's visions involves his nurse speaking Hebrew—though she insists that this is impossible, since she is Italian.) If *Perestroika*, the second half of *Angels*, is less dramatically effective than *Millennium Approaches*, it is largely because Kushner was not sure what to do with the Angel once she arrived. How could he be, when redemption is necessarily prospective, something that is always just about to happen?

The visitation of the Angel, in this context, constitutes a rebuttal of modern Jewish progressivism by a much older kind of Jewish messianism. The metaphysical perspective proves to be more comprehensive, and paradoxically more humane, than Louis's liberal humanism, which cannot reckon with the world's true darkness and suffering. Indeed, the title of the play is spoken by Louis in the course of a speech in which he denies the existence of the metaphysical: "There are no gods here, no ghosts and spirits in America, there are no angels in America, no spiritual past, no racial past, there's only the political."

That line comes in the act titled "Democracy in America," in which Louis and Belize, an African American nurse who is Prior's former lover, argue about the grounds for political hope in the United States. Belize finds himself opposed to Louis's brand of politics, once again on the grounds that liberalism is too shallow to take stock of human realities. But for Belize, it is the fact of race that undermines Louis's faith in the triumph of politics. For this faith, Kushner correctly suggests, is a product of the particular experience that Jews have had in America.

Louis is by no means an optimist about American politics, but he does possess the Jewish liberal's fundamental faith in the American difference. "Why has democracy succeeded in America?" begins his speech in Act Three, Scene Two of *Millennium Approaches*, and he goes on to explain that it is because there is no such thing as an American racial essence. "The Jews of Europe were never Europeans, just a small problem. Facing the monolith. But here there are so many small problems . . . the monolith is missing," he argues.

As far as Jewish experience goes, this is entirely accurate: Jews were able to assimilate in the United States because there was no racial-religious monolith impeding their entry. But as Belize goes on to point out, the reason why Jews don't see the American racial monolith, which is whiteness, is that they are inside it. Black Americans cannot sustain the same blissful ignorance. Ironically, even in this scene, the black character is made to perform an educative function for a white character and an implicitly white audience. Several of the black actors and critics interviewed in *The World Only Spins Forward* make this point, and Kushner himself acknowledges it: "I didn't feel tremendously comfortable with the fact that I was writing a contemporary black character," he says. Perhaps it is because the scene is so fraught that Kushner ends up defusing it with a comic exchange of provocations: "Louis Farrakhan!" Louis shouts, to which Belize replies, "Ed Koch!"

Still, the scene is a crucial moment in the play's self-consciousness, and in Louis's self-criticism. Belize is voicing the same rebuttal to Louis that Langston Hughes offers to Ginsberg: "America was never America to me." In obvious ways, the black experience proves the opposite of the Jewish experience. It is a story of the durability of American racism, and of the enormous effort required to budge the country in the direction of justice. Above all, the black experience reminds Jews of the uncomfortable fact that we have thrived in this country in large part because Ashkenazi Jews could assimilate into whiteness. In Europe, Jews were the traditional object of oppression; in America, we found that position already occupied.

This fact created a cognitive dissonance on the Jewish left that persists to this day, as could be seen in the 2018 fight over whether the organizers of the Women's March should disavow Louis Farrakhan for his naked anti-Semitism. (Once again, the 2010s prove to be a continuation of the 1980s.) For the Jewish left, the refusal of some black leaders to do this was especially painful, since it exposed the contradiction at the heart of their political identity. The left, historically, is a coalition of the oppressed, of all the groups damaged by the existing social order. Jews used to be such a group, and in Eastern Europe they naturally took a leading role in left politics. This legacy persisted in the first generation of American Jewish immigrants, poor laborers who suffered from both class and religious oppression.

But in America in the twenty-first century, Jews can no longer plausibly claim to be part of the coalition of the oppressed. The grounds of Jewish politics have shifted; the majority of Jews may still feel themselves to belong "on the left," but really it would be more accurate to describe them as liberals. That is to say, their politics are based on ideas about rights and fairness, not on the experience of powerlessness and the consequent desire to redistribute power. Liberal shibboleths like freedom of speech and due process are still strongly compelling to Jews, because we know that we flourish in societies where we are treated legally and socially as equal individuals, rather than as members of a class or group. And it is our confidence in our status as free individuals that allows us to maintain a communal life that is, compared with that of modern European Jewry, remarkably confident and secure.

Everywhere that liberalism dawned in the nineteenth century, it brought emancipation to the Jews, and enabled an amazing burst of Jewish activity and creativity. The enemies of liberalism recognized the affinity between Jews and liberalism, which is why anti-Semitism became one of the most effective tools of European illiberalism and populism, on both the left and the right. But America was always the exception, the one country where liberalism was so ingrained in the social order that Jews did not have to worry it was about to disappear. The principles of freedom and individualism were written into the Constitution; neither socialism nor fascism took root here, even at the worst moments of the twentieth century. Anti-Semitism, never as bad in America as it had been in the old country, became less and less salient to the lives of Jews after World War II, when it was discredited by association with Nazism.

This state of affairs is indirectly attested in *Angels in America*, which speaks in Jewish accents about Jewish concerns, yet describes itself as "a gay fantasia on national themes." Its Jewishness was not novel or radical enough to be noteworthy. The danger for Jews in Kushner's play lies, rather, in assimilation. This is presaged in the play's first speech, delivered by a rabbi as a eulogy for Louis Ironson's grandmother. The rabbi jokes about the irony of such a woman, a first-generation Jewish immigrant, having a grandchild named Eric ("This is a Jewish name?"). But this kind of assimilation is not what bothers Kushner; rather, what he deplores in the strongest terms is ideological assimilation. To discard the Jewish heritage of liberalism, to come to identify with the powerful and secure—in short, to join the monolith—is the original sin in Kushner's eyes.

That is why he found his perfect villain in Roy Cohn. "I fucking hate traitors," Cohn rages, meaning communists like the Rosenbergs. But in the play's view, it is Cohn who is the ultimate traitor. He is despicable twice over: as a gay man who denies his sexuality and hides his HIV status, and as a Jew who helped to send the Rosenbergs to the electric chair. The play convicts Cohn of forgetting that Jews have a sacred obligation to identify with the powerless—because we were slaves in Egypt, as the Torah says; because we were immigrants like Louis Ironson's grandmother, as the play's rabbi says. "You do not live in America, no such place exists," the rabbi warns, and the warning is necessary precisely because the premise is false. We do live in America, which is why we can forget what it means to be Jewish; and because we can forget, it is a duty to remember. American Jews, one might say, are liberals out of necessity, and left-liberals out of a sense of honor.

But in Trump's America, this traditional Jewish left-liberalism has come under pressure from all sides. The resurgence of anti-Semitism on the so-called alt-right is not, for now, a genuine political danger. It remains a fringe phenomenon, its voice amplified out of all proportion by social media. The mass basis for anti-Semitic politics still does not exist in a country where, according to a 2017 Pew poll, Jews are held in higher regard than any other religious group. (The least liked were Muslims and atheists.)

Still, for most American Jews, the Trump years have been the first time they encountered the existence of real, aggressive anti-Semitism in this country. More worrying than its existence is the way that it has been teasingly countenanced by Trump—in his refusal to condemn the white supremacist marchers in Charlottesville, or in his use of the term "globalist." This is the kind of thing that makes Jews, in particular, feel that the American government is now in the hands of people hostile to Jews and to the liberal order. The parallels with Philip Roth's *The Plot Against America* have been made often: for American Jews, the rise of an authoritarian, anti-Semitic government is the ultimate nightmare. On some subconscious, unadmitted level, we dread the humiliation of discovering that we are no better than those deluded German Jews who thought their patriotism would save them.

So far, however, the danger to the Jews has remained in the realm of the potential, of fears and doubts rather than immediate threats. When Jewish leftists complain that other parts of the left coalition do not take anti-Semitism seriously, they are likely to be met with the response that this is because anti-Semitism is not serious. This answer, which Jews might once have understood, no longer feels accurate to us in the age of Steve Bannon and Richard Spencer. To Jews on the left, the indifference of their fellow leftists is yet another element of the nightmare—the kind of bad dream where no one can hear you scream.

Yet even under Trump, the liberal order in America retains enough vitality, or at least enough inertia, to make the Jews continue to look like winners in American society, rather than losers. (Certainly it would be hard to argue that Farrakhan poses a genuine threat to Jewish well-being.) That is why the association of Jews with power and money continues to find an audience on the left. When supporters of Jeremy Corbyn in the United Kingdom blame Russian assassinations on Israel, or when a DC city councilman says that the Rothschilds control the weather, they are resurrecting very old ideas about sinister Jewish influence. Anti-Zionism is often the key ingredient here; people who put out lists of "neoconservatives" and members of the "Israel

Lobby" during the George W. Bush administration are not likely now to have much sympathy for Jewish feelings of vulnerability and persecution.

This leaves American Jews in a position that our ancestors were all too familiar with: we are unwanted by the left or the right. That is because both political extremes think in terms of groups and classes, and Jews cannot succeed in America on those terms. We will always be a small and dispensable group, more profitable to attack than to defend. It is only when rights mean more than identities—only, that is, in a liberal society—that minorities such as Jews have a chance to flourish. This does not mean that liberalism is a Jewish idea, as its enemies have so often said. It is a universal idea, and preeminently an American idea. But it does mean that the fate of American Jews is tied to the survival of the liberal order. If it fails, no angel is going to come through the ceiling to save us.

Is There Such a Thing
as Jewish Literature?

Is there such a thing as Jewish literature? Surely the answer is
obvious. Go into any bookstore or library, and the Judaica section will be overflowing with books—and that's not to mention
the Jewish authors in the fiction and poetry and history sections.
No wonder Jews take pride in thinking of ourselves as "the people of the book." This designation originates in Islam: the Koran
refers to Jews and Christians, who possess their own scriptures,
as "peoples of the book," and appoints them to a higher place in
society than ignorant pagans. But modern Jews have taken it
over as a peculiarly fitting description, even a title of honor—as
though Jewish culture has a special affinity for books, as though
reading and writing are in some sense constitutive of Jewish
identity.

This is the argument made by the Israeli novelist Amos Oz

and his daughter, the historian Fania Oz-Salzberger, in their book *Jews and Words*. Judaism, they insist, is more than a creed in which all Jews must believe, and it is more than a genetic relationship or an ethnic identity. What defines Jewishness, the Ozes suggest, is a special relationship to texts. Jewish "children were made to inherit not only a faith, not only a collective fate, not only the irreversible mark of circumcision, but also the formative stamp of a library," they write. "Jewish continuity has always hinged on uttered and written words, on an expanding maze of interpretations, debates and disagreements. . . . Ours is not a bloodline but a textline."

Of course, there is some self-flattery in this idea. Every culture has its books, and some have literary traditions even older than the Jews'. This point was driven home to me by a 2013 exhibition of contemporary Chinese art at the Metropolitan Museum, whose title was "Ink Art"—art made with and about the implements of writing. One of the most striking works in the exhibit was "Family Tree," a series of photographs by the artist Zhang Huan, in which he documents the way he inscribed classic Chinese texts in ink on his own face. With each image, the characters grow thicker and harder to read, and the artist's face more deeply dyed, until finally his entire face is an illegible blue mask. It is a brilliant image of the burden of literary tradition— the inheritor of so many texts is eventually submerged by them— but also of the creative and transformative powers of tradition. The blue of the artist's face is an exotic and ambiguous kind of beauty, just as the soul formed by three thousand years of literary tradition takes on a special distinction—one in which deformity and sublimity seem linked.

This was not a Jewish image, but it seemed to me that it easily could have been. It put me in mind of a famous aphorism from Pirkei Avot: "Rabbi Yaakov would say: One who walks along a road and studies, and interrupts his studying to say, 'How beautiful is this tree!,' 'How beautiful is this ploughed field!'—the Torah considers it as if he had forfeited his life." This is likely to strike a modern reader as harshly puritanical: how could it be offensive to God to notice the beauty of God's Creation? The text does not exactly say that we should never notice worldly beauty, but it does make clear that when the world competes with Torah study for our attention, the Torah must win every time. The sacred text is a more intimate and important reflection of God than even the world God created. Textuality is the Jew's most authentic way of encountering the divine.

In her short story "The Pagan Rabbi," Cynthia Ozick offers a provocative fable on this theme. The rabbi of the title, Isaac Kornfeld, begins innocently enough, by starting to notice the beauty of brooks and flowers. But soon he advances to worshipping nature, and finally he falls in love with a Dryad, a pagan tree-spirit, and even has sex with her. ("Scripture," he notes, "does not forbid sodomy with the plants.") He is devastated, however, when he is granted a glimpse of his own soul as the Dryad perceives it. He takes the form of "a quite ugly old man," trudging down the road holding a "huge and terrifying volume" —a tractate of the Talmud. "His cheeks are folded like ancient flags, he reads the Law and breathes the dust." A Jew, Ozick suggests, is spiritually a scholar, wedded to old books, even when he thinks he is achieving communion with Nature. Like the dyed face of Zhang Huan, the Jewish spirit is made of ink, not flesh and blood. When Kornfeld, his love thwarted, commits suicide by hanging himself from a tree, his widow sees it as a just punishment for his sin, which was to elevate the body above the mind, nature above text. "We are not like them," she observes, meaning gentiles. "Their bodies are more to them than ours are to us. Our books are holy, to them their bodies are holy."

For Ozick, being authentically Jewish means choosing text over everything, even life itself. This is a shocking proposition, and she intends it to be: for she is confronting the reader with a conception of Jewishness that the modern world has rendered antiquated, if not offensive. Indeed, the harshness of traditional Jewish education, the way early training in texts rendered the Jewish student alienated from nature and his own body, was one of the main complaints of the Jewish Enlightenment, known as the Haskalah. The pioneering modern Hebrew poet Chaim Nahman Bialik echoed this criticism in his long poem "The Talmud Student," where he describes his fellow young scholars:

> When young I heard these voices,
> I saw these mute toilers;

brows furrowed, wide-eyed, pale-faced—
as if begging mercy.
Each furrow and glance—a strangled urge,
a dead spark; they stirred my thoughts;
scalded, my heart recoiled,
but remembering their cry at night,
like men being slaughtered,
I cried out:
God! What are they dying for?

Despite such ardent protests, however, Ozick insists, not so much pessimistically as fatalistically, that the Jewish connection with texts is too deep to be erased by any program of modernization. When the Ozes make the same argument, it takes on a more hopeful cast; for if Jewishness is constituted by a particular relationship to texts, then the form of Jewish culture remains even after its content has fragmented. Today, Jews are divided between Israel and America, between Hebrew and English, between Orthodoxy and secularism, to name just the most prominent lines of fracture. But we are still united, the Ozes believe, by textuality—the sense that reading and writing are the most authentic way of relating to the world. "Jewish parenting," they write, "had, perhaps still has, a unique academic edge. Being a parent meant performing some level of text-based teaching."

The classic example of this ideal can be found in the Passover Seder, when we read about the Four Sons—the wise, the wicked, the simple, and the one who doesn't know how to ask a question.

The wise son, the good Jewish son, is defined by his intellectual curiosity: "What does the wise son say? 'What are the testimonials, statutes and laws the Lord our God commanded you?'" And his reward is to be initiated into the knowledge of Jewish law: "You should tell him about the laws of Pesach, that one may eat no dessert after eating the Pesach offering." This is Jewish education as it is supposed to be: asking questions and receiving answers, a passing along of knowledge from generation to generation.

The question, however, is whether education remains Jewish when it has stopped asking about the "testimonials, statutes and laws" that make up Judaism. Is there an identifiably Jewish style of thought, which marks its practitioner as belonging to Jewish tradition even when he is not consciously engaged with that tradition? This question became a central one for Jewish culture starting in the eighteenth century, when the process of Jewish emancipation began. For the first time, in parts of Europe, it became possible for Jews to contribute their intellectual powers not to traditional Jewish study, but to secular subjects like philosophy, medicine, science, and literature.

Just how exhilarating this change was for Jewish intellectuals can be seen in the remarkable *Autobiography* of Solomon Maimon, who lived in the second half of the eighteenth century. Maimon—who took that name in honor of Maimonides, the philosopher who inspired him—was born in what he describes as a miserably backward Jewish village in Lithuania. He was a precocious child who displayed an early curiosity about all kinds of subjects, from painting to astronomy. Yet he remarks bitterly that all of these pursuits were forbidden by the traditional Jewish culture in which he grew up. In that culture, Maimon explains, the only legitimate subject of study was the Talmud, and the only possible aspiration for a gifted boy was to become a rabbi. (A gifted girl, of course, was not even allowed that much.) Maimon dramatizes his predicament with a story:

> I had from childhood a great inclination and talent for drawing. True, I had in my father's house never a chance of seeing a work of art, but I found on the title-page of some Hebrew books woodcuts of foliage, birds, and so forth. I felt great pleasure in these woodcuts, and made an effort to imitate them with a bit of chalk or charcoal. What however strengthened this inclination in me still more was a Hebrew book of fables, in which the personages who play their part in the fables—the animals—were represented in such woodcuts. I copied all the figures with the greatest exactness. My father admired indeed my skill in this, but rebuked me at the same time in these words: "You want to become a painter? You are to study the Talmud, and become a rabbi. He who understands the Talmud, understands everything."

The story Maimon tells in his *Autobiography* is of his gradual revolt against this kind of intellectual tyranny, and his escape from Jewish orthodoxy and superstition into the fresh air of the European Enlightenment. This involved a difficult process of self-education, including teaching himself to read German, which he did by figuring out that the position of the letters in the German alphabet was similar to their position in the Hebrew alphabet. Maimon's introduction to secular philosophy, he writes, came when he entered a shop where the pages of a book on metaphysics were being used to wrap sticks of butter; he managed to convince the shop owner to sell him the book instead.

Finally, after exploring Jewish spiritual movements like Kabbalism and Hasidism and finding them all wanting, Maimon resolved to leave Lithuania and head for Berlin—the capital of the German Enlightenment, and a place where Jews like Moses Mendelssohn were managing to find a place in secular philosophy. It took him several tries to establish himself in Berlin, and he spent years wandering from city to city, living on charity or else starving. In time, he did achieve the reputation he hoped for as a philosopher—his crowning moment came when Immanuel Kant himself announced that no one had understood his work better than Maimon. Still, cut off from traditional Jewish society and unable to find a place for himself in gentile society, Maimon lived an unhappy and unsettled life, and died young. In a book of reminiscences compiled after his death, his friends noted that when studying a difficult mathematical or philosophical work, he would instinctively fall into the traditional rocking and chanting he learned while studying the Talmud as a boy. It is a poignant image of the Jewish intellectual translated into a non-Jewish context, yet never really losing the signature of his origins.

Is a Jewish intellectual still doing something Jewish when he studies Kant instead of the Talmud? Solomon Maimon would not have thought so. For him, the whole point of the Enlightenment was that it meant leaving parochial identities behind and joining in the universally human. And certainly there are areas of intellectual activity where the mind operates independently of its biography: science, above all, which is the pursuit of objective truth about reality. When the Nazis called Einstein's theory of relativity "Jewish science," they were denying that basic objectivity—as if the reality observed by Aryans and the one observed by Jews were irreducibly different, or worse, as if there was something in the Jewish mind that made honest scientific inquiry impossible.

So there is something problematic about the idea that it is possible to be Jewish in form, in style, in habit and manner of thought, without being actually Jewish in content and subject matter. If a mind is trained to study the Talmud, we have no problem calling it a Jewish mind; if a mind is trained to study physics, and it happens to belong to a Jew, is it still a Jewish mind? Or, to take another example, what if the mind is that of a composer? In his landmark book *Jerusalem*, Moses Mendelssohn insisted that it was possible to be both a modern thinker and an Orthodox Jew. This was his advice to his fellow Jews: "Adapt yourselves to the morals and the constitution of the land to which you have been removed; but hold fast to the religion of your fathers too. Bear both burdens as well as you can! . . . remain unflinchingly at the post which Providence has assigned to you, and endure everything that happens to you as your lawgiver foretold long ago."

But this double burden, being German and being Jewish, turned out to be heavier than Mendelssohn's own children wanted to bear. Many of them converted to Christianity, and all of his grandchildren were raised as Christians. One of those grandchildren was Felix Mendelssohn-Bartholdy, who became famous in part for his production of Christian sacred music. Mendelssohn identified himself as a Christian artist. Surely, however, the grandson of Moses Mendelssohn remained in some senses— by inheritance, by family background, by culture—also a Jewish artist?

And yet, in the nineteenth century, the idea that Mendelssohn was a Jewish composer was not a compliment or an interesting subject for inquiry. It was, rather, the charge leveled against him by musical anti-Semites, who refused to believe that a Jew could ever truly enter into the spirit of German music. That is the argument made by Richard Wagner in his notorious essay "Judaism in Music":

> [Mendelssohn] has shown us that a Jew may have the amplest
> store of specific talents, may own the finest and most varied
> culture, the highest and the tenderest sense of honour—yet
> without all these pre-eminences helping him, were it but one
> single time, to call forth in us that deep, that heart-searching
> effect which we await from Art because we know her capable

thereof, because we have felt it many a time and oft, so soon as once a hero of our art has, so to say, but opened his mouth to speak to us.

A Jew, Wagner is certain, can never be a "hero" of art because he can never escape Jewishness: "The Jew speaks the language of the nation in whose midst he dwells from generation to generation, but he speaks it always as an alien." In other words, Wagner is championing the idea that a Jewish mind is always identifiable by its products, that there is some essence of Jewishness that makes Mendelssohn a Jewish artist despite his Christianity. And this Jewishness is, of course, not just different but inferior: "What issues from the Jews' attempts at making Art, must necessarily therefore bear the attributes of coldness and indifference, even to triviality and absurdity; and in the history of Modern Music we can but class the Judaic period as that of final unproductivity, of stability gone to ruin." This idea was not confined to Wagner's essays, but even made its way into his operas. In *Der Meistersinger von Nuremberg*, there is a portrait of a bad composer named Beckmesser, whose incompetent, tone-deaf songs demonstrate all the musical disabilities Wagner associates with the Jews.

Clearly, it is problematic to speak of Jewish music. The expression has an ugly history, and it involves us in all kinds of quandaries about Jewish difference. But what about Jewish literature? Is there some quality or essence that unites different forms of literary expression by Jews, across barriers of time and language and culture? To put it more concretely: do a story in German by Franz Kafka, an essay in English by Susan Sontag, and a novel in Hebrew by Amos Oz all belong in the same category? What if we add to that category the Hebrew Bible, the Talmud, and the medieval commentaries of Rashi? Is there any meaningful sense in which these are all Jewish works, other than the fact that they were all written by Jews?

One possible answer to this question is that there is something distinctive about the way Jews relate to texts. If textual study is the core of Judaism—and historically that is exactly what a Jewish education meant—then perhaps a deep involvement with texts is enough to make those who practice it part of Jewish tradition. This idea has been popular among modern American Jewish intellectuals, who have often taken intellectuality itself to be a form of Jewish practice. Harold Rosenberg, the art critic who was a charter member of the New York intellectuals, proudly remarked that "For two thousand years, the main energies of Jewish communities have gone into the mass production of intellectuals." The implication is that a Jew who spent his life analyzing Talmudic debates and a Jew who spent his life analyzing the poems of T. S. Eliot or the novels of Henry James are essentially doing the same thing. Both are engaged in the Jewish activity of interpretation, the discovery of meanings in texts.

This is a reassuring idea for an assimilated American Jew, since it seems to make it possible to be authentically Jewish without knowing anything in particular about Judaism. Obviously, the very activity of literary criticism can't be considered distinctively Jewish. But perhaps there are particular forms of interpretation that have roots in Jewish tradition; perhaps Jewishness is not so much a way of writing as a way of reading. The only way to answer that question, however, is to look at canonical Jewish commentaries and interpreters, to see what kind of role interpretation has traditionally played in Judaism.

Take, for example, the way the rabbis of the Talmud interpret the Purim story, from the book of Esther. In chapter 6 of Esther, we read about how King Ahasuerus, unable to sleep one night, orders his servant to read to him from the royal book of chronicles. He happens to listen to a passage about how Mordecai, the uncle of Queen Esther, once foiled a plot against the king's life. Realizing that Mordecai has never been rewarded for this service, the king asks Haman for advice: what should he do for a man he wishes to honor? Haman, thinking that he must be that man, advises the king to dress him in royal robes and the royal crown and let him ride the royal horse through the streets of the capital. Very well, the king agrees: all this must be done for Mordecai, and Haman must personally lead the horse, proclaiming, "thus shall it be done unto the man whom the king delights to honor."

This incident marks the turning point in the drama of the book of Esther. Haman, who has been plotting to murder Mordecai and with him all the Jews of the Persian Empire, finds himself forced to honor Mordecai instead. Soon, thanks to Esther's intervention, his plans against the Jews will also be thwarted. When the rabbis of the Talmud come to recount this moment in the story, they take such delight in Haman's humiliation that they add new details, not found in the biblical text, in order to heighten and prolong it. For instance, before Mordecai can mount the king's horse, he informs Haman that he must visit the bathhouse and trim his hair—"for," he says, "it is not proper conduct to use the king's garments in this state." In the meantime, however, Esther has sent messengers to all the bathhouses in the city, ordering them to close. So Haman has no choice but to do the job himself, as the Talmud records: "He took Mordecai into the bathhouse and washed him, and he went and brought scissors from his house and trimmed his hair. While he was trimming his hair he injured himself and sighed. Mordecai said to him: Why do you sigh? Haman said to him: The man whom the king had once regarded above all his other ministers is now made a bathhouse attendant and a barber."

The places have been reversed: instead of Mordecai being ordered to bow before Haman, Haman has to perform the menial task of cutting Mordecai's hair. But Mordecai gets in one further jab: "Wicked man," he tells Haman, "were you not once the barber of the village of Kartzum? For it was taught: Haman was the barber of the village of Kartzum for twenty-two years." Now, there is nothing about Haman being a barber in the book of

Esther. This is a gratuitous insult to his social status, designed to further his humiliation. It reads very much as if the rabbis were rubbing it in, inventing new ordeals for Haman in order to glory in the defeat of the Jews' worst enemy. But it is significant that the Talmud itself does not believe that it is adding to or interfering with the biblical text. Rather, the detail about Haman being a barber is something that was "taught." To be valid, any addition to the text must be not an invention, but a genuine fact handed down from time immemorial.

This happens even more dramatically when the rabbis reach the line "Thus shall it be done to the man whom the king delights to honor." In Tractate Megillah, the rabbis explain:

> As Haman was taking Mordecai along the street of Haman's house, Haman's daughter was standing on the roof and saw the spectacle. She thought to herself that the one who is riding on the horse must be her father, and the one walking before him must be Mordecai. She then took a chamber pot and cast its contents onto the head of her father, whom she mistakenly took as Mordecai. When Haman raised his eyes, she saw that he was her father. In her distress, she fell from the roof to the ground and died.

This is a wonderfully gross example of literary vengeance. The humiliation of Haman already implicit in the whole situation is compounded by having him covered in excrement, and then killing off his daughter to boot. But how do the rabbis justify this addition to the biblical story? The answer is given by

Rav Sheshet, who points to one verse from the original book of Esther, which reads, "Haman hastened to his house, mourning, and having his head covered." Now, in the original context, it is plain that his mourning and disguise are simply because he is embarrassed at having been seen in public as Mordecai's inferior. But Sheshet seizes on the biblical phrasing and seeks to expand on it. If Haman is "mourning," surely it is because someone has died; and if he has his head covered, surely it is because there is something objectionable there? The story of the chamber pot and the dead daughter fits the bill perfectly.

This is not to say that the story was invented to meet the requirements of the verse. Perhaps the story was made up first and the verse adduced later to give it legitimacy. But Rav Sheshet's remark does give us a vivid and fascinating example of one kind of rabbinic interpretation or midrash. A biblical story is not necessarily complete; by attending to the exact words and expressions it uses, we can extrapolate other details that fit its spirit and intention. This kind of midrash is seen not as violating the integrity of the biblical text, but as completing it.

At the same time, midrash can also end up contradicting the biblical text, if for some reason the rabbis find the Bible's account objectionable on moral or theological grounds. Take, for instance, the brief account in Genesis 35 about Reuben, the oldest of Jacob's twelve sons: "And it came to pass, while Israel dwelt in that land, that Reuben went and he lay with Bilhah, his father's concubine, and Israel heard." That is the whole story, a single verse. It is not mentioned again until the end of the book of Genesis, when the dying Jacob curses Reuben: "Unstable as water, you shalt not excel; because you went up to your father's bed, and defiled it; he went up to my couch." There would seem to be no ambiguity in this brief story: Reuben had sex with Bilhah, which is practically incest, since she was his father's bedmate. But when Rashi, the great medieval commentator, came to annotate this verse, he explained that Reuben did no such thing. Actually, what he did was simply to move his father's bed, taking it out of Bilhah's tent in order to put it into the tent of his own mother, Leah, Jacob's first wife. As Rashi writes:

> As a result of the fact that Reuben disturbed the location of Jacob's bed, Scripture treats him as if he had lain with her [Bilhah]. And why did Reuben disturb and desecrate Jacob's couch? Because when Rachel died, Jacob took his bed, which had regularly been situated in the tent of Rachel, and not in other tents, and put it into the tent of Bilhah. Reuben came and demanded satisfaction for the insult to his mother [Leah]. He said, "If my mother's sister was a rival of my mother, how should my mother's sister's handmaiden be a rival of my mother?" This is why he disturbed the location of Jacob's bed.

In this way, Rashi evacuates the literal meaning of the biblical text. Reuben, the patriarch's son, namesake of one of the twelve tribes, was surely too righteous a man to do something as sinful as sleep with his father's concubine; it follows that this cannot be what the Bible meant. It must have meant something else, and the story Rashi offers reflects much better on Reuben. Now he is motivated not by transgressive lust, but by a noble desire to protect his mother's rights. This kind of midrash is very free with the literal meaning of the biblical text, but only in the service of what it sees as a higher kind of truth. It tells us what the Bible ought to have meant, if it is to be the kind of book piety expects it to be. The idea that the biblical authors were less pious than their rabbinic readers, that the Bible countenances a lot of behavior that would have appeared sinful to later versions of Judaism, is a modern insight that the rabbis do not share.

To look at these classic examples of Jewish exegesis is to recognize that, despite Harold Rosenberg's implication, there is no real similarity between what the rabbis meant by interpretation and what a contemporary, secular literary critic means by it. When the rabbis interpret a sacred text, they do so in a paradoxical way. They are at the same time far more reverential toward it than we are toward any literary text, and also far more free and creative in their reading. That is because a biblical story is, in the traditional view, authored by God, and a text of divine origin must be as infinite as its author. It is impossible to read anything into such a text, because it already contains every conceivable meaning. With a literary text, on the other hand, the critic's interpretation must stay within the boundaries defined by genre, language, and authorial intention. A reader of Henry James who invented new details in the life of Isabel Archer, in *The Portrait of a Lady*, the way Rav Sheshet invented new details in the Esther story, would be considered a very irresponsible critic.

Is it possible, then, for a modern, secular Jewish writer to appropriate this tradition, to make use of it in an authentic way? One answer is provided by the work of Walter Benjamin, whose essays on literature and culture are some of the foundational texts of modernism. Benjamin's relationship to his own Jewish heritage was problematic: raised in a secular home, he knew almost nothing about Judaism as a religion, and he identified strongly with the German literary tradition. Yet his friendship with Gershom Scholem, who would go on to become the leading modern scholar of Jewish mysticism, introduced Benjamin to some of the key concepts of Jewish tradition—including the idea of God as an author who used language to create the Torah and the world. In his essay "The Task of the Translator," Benjamin draws on this tradition to develop a radical theory of language and translation. A text, he writes, might never be successfully interpreted by human beings, but in principle it remains interpretable, because there is a perspective—God's perspective—from which the fullness of its meaning can be seen.

This is a frankly mystical conception of language, and it has a deep affiliation with the way the rabbis read Scripture. For the rabbis, too, the interpretability of texts was guaranteed by their divinity. Benjamin's radicalism lies in the way he extends this interpretability even to human texts, to works of secular literature. All language, not just sacred language, has a divine and infinite dimension, so that translation becomes a kind of priestly task. The difference is that while the rabbis had confidence that their own interpretations were authorized by God—that what they said about Haman and Reuben was true—a secular interpreter can have no such certainty.

What Benjamin is dramatizing is the rupture of a tradition. He places himself in the lineage of Jewish textual interpreters, not simply because he is a Jew who happens to be a literary critic, but because he takes seriously the metaphysical principles that governed Jewish exegesis. Yet he speaks as one who has inherited the form of that tradition without its content. He knows that the importance of interpretation is infinite, but he is no longer sure that he is actually capable of finding a correct interpretation. Elsewhere in Benjamin's work, this principle is extended from actual literary texts to all of creation. In an explicitly mystical early essay, "On Language as Such and the Language of Man," he writes, "There is no event or thing in either animate or inanimate nature that does not in some way partake of language." A kabbalist might say the same thing, but the traditional Jewish mystic believed that it was possible to "read" the words of nature, because they were the words—literally, the Hebrew letters—with which God created the universe. For Benjamin, this communication is broken: we live in a world constituted by a language we cannot read.

This has a very Kafkaesque sound, and it is no coincidence that Benjamin became one of Franz Kafka's early critical champions. Both emerged from the German-speaking Jewish bourgeoisie in the early twentieth century, a time of deep crisis in the

Jewish world. So it makes sense that Kafka, like Benjamin, was especially attuned to images of fractured tradition and blocked interpretation. These ideas are everywhere in his fiction, but probably their most vivid and celebrated expression comes in the section of *The Trial* known as "Before the Law." In this episode, a priest tells Joseph K., the man wanted for an unknown crime, an ancient story about a man who seeks admittance to the Law. But the door to the Law is guarded by a door-keeper, who refuses to let him in. The man spends his entire life waiting for the door to be opened, but it never is. Finally, when he is dying, he asks the door-keeper why he has never seen another person ask to be allowed in. "No one but you could gain admittance through this door, since this door was intended only for you," the door-keeper replies. "I am now going to shut it."

In this story, Kafka never explains just what "the Law" is or what it might mean to gain admittance to it. But it is unmistakable that the Law, the Torah, is the center of Judaism, the thing that pious Jews had studied for generations. Kafka's pilgrim, unable to find his way into the Law, resembles the modern Jew who has no point of entry to Jewish tradition. The Jewish resonance of this parable is made almost explicit in the following pages, when Joseph K. engages the priest in a long and fruitless conversation, attempting to interpret the story and figure out what it is trying to say. "The scriptures are unalterable," the priest remarks, "and the comments [on them] often enough merely express the commentator's bewilderment." This is a scene of failed interpretation, of a Scripture that refuses to give up its secrets. Yet by engaging in the process of dialectic, asking questions and ruling out alternatives, Joseph K. seems to be enacting, in a failed, parodic form, the kind of argument that fuels scriptural analysis in the Talmud.

In traditional midrash, Walter Benjamin pointed out, story "lies down at the feet of doctrine": the interpreter reads texts in order to make them conform with religious truth, as with Rashi's interpretation of the Reuben story. But in Kafka, Benjamin went on, story, "having crouched down, unexpectedly cuffs doctrine with a weighty paw." This resistance to or refusal of interpretation is what makes all of Kafka's work read like a parable with a missing key, an allegory of something that no one can quite name. And this situation, which is Jewish in origin and in conception, proved to be so universal an experience in the twentieth century that Kafka's name was turned into an adjective in order to name it. As always, the local dimension of literature proves to be not an enemy of the universal, but the surest way of reaching the universal.

Does this mean that the only authentic Jewish literature today is literature about the failure of tradition? That would be too absolute and pessimistic a conclusion. Rather, the case of Kafka suggests that what makes literature Jewish is its decision to engage with Jewish texts and vocabularies, even in a negative way. Doing this does not require an extensive knowledge of Jewish tradition, which neither Benjamin nor Kafka possessed, but it does require an instinct for finding the elements in that tradition which can be used, or even misused, in order to communicate a modern truth. Jewish literature is what happens every time a writer tries to make a place for himself or herself in that ancient lineage.

Acknowledgments

I am grateful to the publications where the following essays first appeared, usually in a somewhat different form:

Battersea Review: "Night Thoughts"

Jewish Review of Books: "Non-Jewish Jews: Rosa Luxemburg and Isaac Deutscher"

The New Republic: "Seamus Heaney and the Question of Goodness," "Stefan Zweig at the End of the World," and "The Book of Psalms"

The New Yorker: "Kay Ryan: The Less Deceived"

Poetry: "Extension of the Domain of Struggle" and "The Poetry of World and the Poetry of Earth"

Sewanee Review: "The Faith of Christian Wiman"

Tablet: "Angels of Liberalism"

Index

Index